The ELC: An Early Childhood Learning Community at Work

THE ELC: AN EARLY CHILDHOOD LEARNING COMMUNITY AT WORK

HEATHER BRIDGE, LORRAINE MELITA, AND PATRICIA ROIGER

Open SUNY Textbooks
Geneseo

CONTENTS

ACKNOWLEDGMENTS

From the very start, the Early Learning Community (ELC) was a collaborative venture that would not have existed without extensive interaction between many special individuals. As a group, the authors are grateful to one another for committing time, knowledge, and skills over several years to work in the ELC and contribute to this book in different ways. We take responsibility for the views expressed which are not associated with any setting or agency that participated in the ELC but are solely the provenance of the authors.

For each of us, there are significant mentors, namely Dr. Christine O'Hanlon, the late Doctors, Harriet Cuffaro and Van Burd, each of whom had a profound impact on the development of our critical thinking about early childhood education, and so influenced the shape of the ELC. Colleagues must be recognized, namely Dr. Emilie Kudela and Beth Elberson, who emphasized the importance of collaboration between the college and local preschool agencies involved in early childhood teacher education programs. Media staff and graduate students played a vital role in supporting teacher candidates' use of technology. These individuals include Dawn Van Hall, Hailey Ruoff, Justin Stewart, Loren Leonard, Steven Marstall, Bryant Withers, Kristen Jones and Matt Jones. Professionals in the Office of Research and Sponsored Programs, namely Glen Clarke and Amy Henderson-Harr, were pivotal in helping the authors clarify goals and procedures in the grant submission process and ensuring all requirements were itemized. Joe Ziegler, at the New York State Office of Children and Family Services (NYSOCFS) was a strong advocate of the ELC and faithfully attended each of our ELC professional development conferences. John Beecher in the Finance Office provided thorough oversight in making sure grant funds were spent well and grant progress reports were submitted to the State in a timely manner.

We would like to show our appreciation to the many extraordinary administrators and educators in varied preschool agencies who participated in the ELC. There are too many to name individually, but we would like to convey here what an honor it was to work with all administrators and educators in preschool settings in Cortland County. Those administrators and educators showed enormous courage in their willingness to participate in the ELC. They graciously opened their classroom doors to us, and agreed to investigate their own teaching challenges in support of improving early childhood teaching approaches. The goal now, is to align educators' practice during Practicum, with teacher education Standards, to benefit teacher candidates' professional preparation.

Thank you to all early childhood teacher candidates who participated in the ELC, and worked in teams of educators and in field placement classrooms during Practicum. Teacher candidates' ability to form enquiring professional relationships with senior educators, together with the extra work they completed in the ELC, was often remarkable.

We owe enormous gratitude to our families who have supported us through this long and eventful journey. We thank them for giving us time and encouragement to see the venture through. John Bridge generously provided us with constructive and scholarly feedback. Martin Tucker must be acknowledged for the highly creative work he did in producing visuals to illustrate chapters in the book. Many thanks also to Bob Nichols, Ed Triana, and Antonio Triana for the constant patience and understanding they showed throughout the ELC project.

Thank you to our peer reviewers, Dr. Jeanne Galbraith and Diane Richards for their constructive feedback.

Finally, thank you to our editor, Nancy Oliveri, who worked to improve the clarity and flow of this book, and to Allison Brown and her team for their support and expertise through the editing process.

FOREWORD

When I think of teamwork, I am reminded of a demonstration that I once saw. The presenter had a pile of pencils. He picked up a pencil, put it in one hand, and with a dramatic snap, he had broken it in half. He then went on to attempt to break a bundle of pencils. Of course, they would not break. The message he hoped to convey to us with this simple exercise? Together we are stronger.

This was the driving concept behind a project I participated in over the course of four semesters. The Early Learning Community (ELC) was a collaborative effort between a college, a Child Care Council, and local child care programs. With a grant from the New York State Office of Children and Families (NYS OCFS), the project leaders recruited team leaders from the college and from the community. Each team leader worked with an undergraduate early childhood teacher candidate, a teacher, and a teacher assistant in a local early childhood program, and when possible, the director of the program, too, during a practicum field experience.

Each team designed an action research project. Teams started by asking a question or stating a problem they faced in their classroom. For example, "How can we improve behavior in a class of 3-year-old boys?" Then the team researched their question.

Video equipment, purchased with grant funds, was used to document and explore the research question. Through video analysis, and exploring their own perceptions, the team members started to polish and sharpen their particular question, and develop a research topic.

The teacher candidates used their access to the college library to look for literature related to their topic, and then shared that with the team. After reviewing the literature, the team came up with a strategy to try, and a tool to evaluate their strategy. After implementation and evaluation, conclusions were drawn, and the teacher candidates created presentations to share with all the other teams.

So how were we stronger together? First, through collaborating with the child care programs, and the Child Care Council, the college was able to access the NYS OFCS grant. Then, each team became stronger because it combined with a team leader, with a teacher candidate, and with program staff during the practicum field placement experience. Each team member brought his or her own strengths to the team:

- As organizers and facilitators, the team leaders could give feedback and direct the flow of conversations with an outsider's eye, as he or she did not work within the program.
- Teacher candidates had fresh, new ideas, newly acquired in college classes. They also had easy access to the college library and were often more comfortable using the video recording technology. These days, everyone carries recording equipment in their pocket. But during the program, this was the exception.
- Program staff brought years of experience and practical knowledge to the team. They were also the ones who were consistently present in the classrooms, so they often saw things that a team leader and teacher candidate did not.

Finally, we were stronger because we reviewed current research in published books and journals. We had the strengths of the whole Early Childhood field behind us. Together, we were able to improve practice in the classrooms with an eye toward helping all early childhood staff to work more effectively, understanding how children learned. So together, we *are* stronger.

Anne Withers is the Child Care Resource & Referral Director for a Child Development Council in New York. She has been working in the Early Childhood Field for 33 years in schools, nursery schools, child care centers, family child care, and child care resource and referral. Anne enjoys solving problems, helping families, and watching child care providers grow and learn along with their children.

PREFACE

As authors, we chose the subject for this book because of what early childhood teacher candidates told us about their confusion between the theory they were taught in college methods classes, and, the teaching practices they often experienced during the Practicum field placement. We became interested in this subject because the teacher candidates were questioning, as good teacher candidates do, a troubling disconnect between early childhood theory and associated practice in classrooms. We were motivated to write this book because we wanted to share our model of professional development, designed to support both pre-service teacher candidates and, in-service educators together, during the Practicum field placement. Our lead author secured a grant to investigate these concerns and to implement a new professional development model designed to overcome them. The substance of this book reminds all of us, that in early childhood education, educators' change through professional development, for improved practice that benefits children's learning, is a constant.

The idea to write this book began a year after the grant ended. We were not quite done with all that had been accomplished and wanted others in the early childhood field to learn about our professional development model, which we know is still highly relevant today. It has taken us approximately seven years to complete the book. We overcame many challenges during writing, not the least of which was distance. The lead author now lives in the United Kingdom while the other two authors live in the United States. Technology was extremely helpful throughout the writing process. Skype was the best way for us to "see" each other regularly and to work out differences and correct inconsistencies.

As friends and writers, we grew in our understanding of teacher candidates' ability to ask questions that would lead them towards becoming better educators in the future. The Early Learning Community (ELC) used an Action Research model, that assists educators in using a wide variety of investigative, analytical and evaluative, research methods designed to diagnose problems or weaknesses in their classrooms — whether organizational, academic, or instructional—and help educators develop practical solutions to address them quickly and efficiently (https://www.edglossary.org/action-research/). Further, we incorporated into Action Research, collaboration between early childhood agencies, technology, literature, and conference presentations to bring about professional growth in teacher candidates in college, educators in practicum field placements, administrators in preschools and in ourselves, as college faculty members and community experts.

The structure of this book is organized into three parts. In Part I, the initial challenges that stimulated the idea of the ELC are described. An explanation of the stages in setting up the ELC is provided to guide our audience, should they choose to replicate this model. In Part II, six case studies that represent common teaching challenges experienced by teacher candidates during Practicum illustrate the ELC in action. In Part III, participants' findings about the ELC, along with conclusions and recommendations for future early childhood professional development programs are made.

We acknowledge the scope of the ELC was limited in that it operated within a small rural area of NYS and in a restricted number of classrooms. As far as we know, the ELC has not been replicated elsewhere. However, the ELC does provide compelling evidence of educators' improved teaching practice, achieved when agencies concerned with early childhood teacher preparation programs, collaborate across traditional boundaries.

AUDIENCE

Throughout the writing of this book our intended audience was often at the forefront of our minds. We aimed to show the audience how the ELC professional development model is distinct from others that existed in NYS and why our book is worth reading. In 2015, collaboration between NYS Early Childhood Advisory Council, NYS Head Start Collaboration Office, NYS Education Department's Office of Early Learning and NYS Association for the Education of Young Children identified their principal professional development audience as early childhood administrators and teachers. A series of published briefs on specified curriculum topics Pre-K through 3rd grade, supported teaching strategies that reinforced NYS Learning Standards and Common Core Learning outcomes and thereby aimed to secure children's success at each grade level.

By contrast, our book presents a unique "upside-down" model of early childhood professional development. The notion of the ELC started when college faculty listened and responded to teacher candidates' concerns about differences between what they learned in college methods courses and what they sometimes experienced in Practicum placements that resulted in them not being able to carry out required assignments. The focus of the ELC is therefore fixed in local early childhood Practicum classrooms, where teacher candidates and educators work to improve teaching and standard alignment challenges they currently face in the classroom. Our early childhood audience, consisting of pre-service teacher candidates, in-service teachers, classroom assistants, pre-school administrators, college faculty, researchers of learning communities and early childhood policy makers is intentionally broad to illustrate how varied groups of early childhood educators, based in different settings, can undertake professional development together in teams. The aims of the ELC were to: (1) build professional development connections between early childhood educators in different agencies involved with Practicum; (2) improve and align educators' practice in Practicum placements with NAEYC Standards (2009) used at the College; (3) demonstrate the impact of the ELC on the professional learning of team participants and on children in Practicum placements. It is imperative therefore, that our broad audience understands the working of the ELC, and the different roles they can each play in using and promoting it.

PART I: SETTING UP THE EARLY LEARNING COMMUNITY (ELC)

1. BUILDING BLOCKS FOR THE ELC

The ELC illustrates how teacher candidates and educators together undertake professional development by creating case studies of their Practicum placement. Case studies have notable strengths because, as stated by Stake (1995, p.1), they facilitate the exploration of rich, contextual information about specific challenges in each classroom and reveal why educators' practice is as it is. Case Studies used with Action Research allow for the investigation and improvement of real teaching challenges in Practicum placement classrooms.

The ELC is aimed at educators becoming life-long learners who are empowered to investigate positive change in their own teaching. Rooted in children's development, the ELC equips educators with a set of professional skills that enable them to implement developmentally-appropriate, research-backed, teaching strategies that are responsive to children's current learning needs. The development of educators' teaching skills in their own classrooms is at the very heart of effective and reflective professional development for it is on this premise that each child's appropriate opportunities for development and learning rest. We hope our efforts may inspire the audience to create similar early learning communities in their early childhood settings.

Starting Point: Teacher Candidates' Concerns in Practicum

A key characteristic of effective early childhood teacher education programs is demonstrated by alignment between the educational theory taught to teacher candidates in college courses, and the teaching practices those teacher candidates encounter during Practicum field placements.

Concurrently with the Practicum, teacher candidates at the college took a curriculum development course, and an assessment course, aimed at teaching 3 -5-year old children. During Practicum, teacher candidates were required to spend at least 75 hours in an early childhood field placement with a certified teacher. By the end of the semester, teacher candidates had to demonstrate satisfactory knowledge, understanding, and use of teacher education standards in their practice and lesson plan assignments they implemented during Practicum.

If the educational theory prescribed in teacher education standards used in teacher education programs and the teaching practices in field placement experiences are not closely aligned, the impact on teacher candidates can raise concern (Gismondi, Haser, 2003; Rust, 2009). Inconsistencies between theory and practice can leave teacher candidates feeling confused about their practice with children in classrooms. On the one hand, teacher candidates are required by their teacher education program to prepare assignments based on teacher education standards to implement during Practicum. On the other hand, the assignments must also accord with sometimes different teaching and care practices they encounter in their Practicum field placements. As a result, teacher candidates can come to believe that the theory taught in college courses, and the teaching practices used in field placements, are unrelated. This belief can perpetuate teacher candidates' use of less effective educational and care practices in classrooms and reduce the quality of learning and development opportunities children experience.

NAEYC Standards Alignment Issues

Since 2002, the National Association for the Education of Young Children (NAEYC) Standards (2009), were used in the college teacher education program and were also used in the ELC. NAEYC is a professional body in the USA, in which widely held truths about the theory, research, and practice that teacher candidates are expected to learn in teacher education programs, concerning the education and care of young children from birth to eight years are articulated. NAEYC standards (2009) can be seen at this link: https://www.naeyc.org/ sites/default/files/globally-shared/downloads/PDFs/our-work/higher-ed/NAEYC-Professional-Preparation-Standards.pdf

The NAEYC Standards (2009) are described as providing "a sustained vision of excellence for programs that prepare teacher candidates to work with young children between the ages of birth to eight years" (Hyson, Tomlinson, & Morris, 2009) and were organized under six Core Standards:

Standard 1: Promoting Child Development and Learning
Standard 2: Building Family and Community Relationships
Standard 3: Observing, Documenting and Assessing to Support Young Children and Families
Standard 4: Using Developmentally Effective Approaches to Connect with Children and Families
Standard 5: Using Content Knowledge to Build Meaningful Curriculum
Standard 6: Becoming a Professional
Table 1.1 NAEYC Core Standards (2009)

Key elements of each core standard highlighted the main aspects of each and expanded on the requirements for teacher candidates in early childhood degree programs. A version of NAEYC Standards (2009) included updates that placed more emphasis on Standard 5, concerning the teaching of content areas in early childhood education, and on Standard 1, concerning provision for the effective inclusion of each child with diverse learning needs in early childhood settings.

In the college early childhood teacher education program, NAEYC Standards (2009) served multiple purposes. They: (1) promoted competence in teacher candidates in the areas of ethics, child development, families, curriculum design, assessment, and professionalism; (2) shaped course assignments and rubrics that promoted focused assessment of teacher candidates' competencies; (3) aligned the teacher education program with requirements for national accreditation; (4) aligned the program with New York State teacher education requirements; and (5) enabled smooth transfer of credit for teacher candidates who moved from community colleges to the teacher education program at the college.

Challenges arose during Practicum over how the "vision of excellence" portrayed in NAEYC Standards (2009) could be turned into reality in Practicum placements. The challenges and their implications are summarized in tables 1.2 and 1.3 below. The term "educator" collectively describes teachers, assistant teachers and administrators who hosted teacher candidates during the Practicum field placement.

Challenges	College Teacher Education Program	Practicum Field Placements	Misalignment
Alignment between Early Childhood theory taught to teacher candidates in college, and conflicting practices they experienced in Practicum settings	Teacher candidates were required to prepare and implement assignments based on NAEYC Standards for Early Childhood Professional Preparation Programs (2009) in Practicum settings	Educators' practice was based on the particular Early Childhood Standards used in their setting	No collaboration existed between college faculty and educators in Practicum settings to ensure alignment existed between teacher candidates' assignments and practice in Practicum settings

Table 1.2: Summary of challenges that existed during Practicum

Implication of Challenges	Early Childhood Program	Practicum Field Placements	Misalignment
Teacher candidates' confusion	Teacher candidates reported confusion over the use of NAEYC Standards for Early Childhood Professional Preparation Programs (2009) theory taught in college and their implementation in Practicum assignments...	...and conflicting practice they saw in Practicum	No collaboration existed between college faculty and educators in Practicum settings regarding consistent implementation of NAEYC Standards for Early Childhood Professional Preparation Programs (2009) during Practicum
Teacher candidates' mistaken perceptions	Teacher candidates commonly believed that Early Childhood theory taught in the teacher education program was unrelated...	...to Early Childhood practice they saw in Practicum	Concern about the quality of teacher candidates' future teaching led to the formation of the Early Learning Community (ELC) designed to improve and align practice in Practicum settings with NAEYC Standards for Early Childhood Professional Preparation Programs (2009)

Table 1.3: Summary of the challenge implications for teacher candidates

Teacher candidates' comments in class discussions and entries in their journals, showed they were often "confused by having to prepare and teach lesson plans aligned with the 2009 NAEYC Standard 5: Using content knowledge to build meaningful curriculum" (page 15) for mathematics, science, social studies and the arts. Their confusion arose from rarely seeing children learning in these content areas in their Practicum classrooms. Other teacher candidates explained that because "literacy was huge in many Practicum classrooms, learning in mathematics, science, social studies and the arts was, by comparison, rarely seen." As a result, teacher candidates found it difficult to assess children's current understanding of concepts in these content areas, and plan and teach required developmentally-appropriate lesson plans. Teacher candidates also said it was difficult to find enough resources to support children's learning of key concepts and skills in each of these content areas.

Teacher candidates' beliefs concerning the disconnect between the early childhood theory they were taught in college courses, and some teaching practices they observed in Practicum, caused concern among early childhood college faculty. Such notions threatened to undermine implementation of NAEYC Standards (2009) in the future, when the teacher candidates became teachers themselves. Teacher candidates were at risk of not using recommended developmentally-appropriate practices (DAP) known to be most beneficial in supporting children's learning in their Practicum placements.

DAP is described by NAEYC in Developmentally Appropriate Practice in Early Childhood Programs Serving Children from Birth Through Age 8 (2009). The purpose of DAP is to promote excellence in early childhood education by providing a framework for best practice. Grounded in both research on child development and learning, and in the knowledge base regarding educational effectiveness, DAP defined the practices that did this best. In addition to the lack of DAP practices in some Practicum settings, educators in the ELC, identified the following teaching areas as particularly challenging: children's ineffectual play; a lack of discrete activities to meet children's individual learning needs; inappropriate management of children's behavior; and insufficient opportunities for physical play.

Building the ELC

The search to find ways to help both teacher candidates and educators improve their teaching in Practicum placements was begun and the opportunity to create an ELC presented itself. An ELC is characterized by Harvard University's Center on the Developing Child: Early Childhood Learning Community Examples. (n.d.). Retrieved from https://developingchild.harvard.edu/collective-change/learning-communities-in-action/

> *"Rapid, breakthrough change cannot happen in the field of early childhood unless people, organizations, and systems learn from each other's successes and failures. This requires a platform for asking and answering questions such as: which interventions work for which populations and why? The Center on the Developing Child facilitates the development of learning communities that provide the means for early childhood innovators to set goals, share results, and cultivate not only leaders, but also new ideas."*

This description accorded with our mission for our ELC. The strengths of Learning Communities, which featured in our ELC design, included goal sharing across agency boundaries, shared leadership, located in classrooms, local accountability, and shared results. At the same time, it was important to recognize obstacles that can exist in learning communities (Smith, 2001). Compliance with participating institutions in learning communities and their existing practice concerning, leadership structures, resource allocation, increased workload, time, curriculum design and willingness to make changes to teaching can all be contentious, may not be supported, and can affect anticipated outcomes. For these reasons, it was essential to find funding to put the ELC on a professional and independent footing.

Funding the ELC

Funding was necessary to secure participants' involvement in the ELC and to pay them for the work they carried out. The New York State's Office of Family and Children's Services (NYSOFCS) Innovative Programs

Initiative awarded the ELC $148,000 to provide professional development opportunities each semester over a two-year period.

The purposes of the grant were to: (1) establish the ELC to improve the alignment of NAEYC Standards between the early childhood curriculum development methods course and the Practicum field experience; (2) encourage teachers and teacher candidates in Practicum to use the same educational and care practices shown to be effective by current research (preferably NAEYC published research) to improve the quality of Practicum experiences offered to Practicum teacher candidates and the quality of childcare and educational services offered to preschool children (aged 3-5 years); (3) create ELC teams that each comprised two early childhood teachers (lead teacher and assistant teacher), a teacher candidate and a team leader that met in Practicum settings weekly for one semester; (4) provide educators and teacher candidates with a team leader to support them carry out and complete the professional development; (5) pay administrators of Practicum settings to provide substitute cover to release educators from their teaching and enable them to attend professional development team meetings each week; (6) pay team leaders, the librarian and the graduate assistant at an hourly rate for their work; (7) purchase books for training workshops, video cameras and digital voice recorders for data collection; (8) provide training to familiarize educators and teacher candidates with the implementation of Action Research in their classrooms to enable them to use it as a long-term problem-solving professional development strategy; (9) purchase materials for an end of semester conference where teams disseminated their Action Research findings.

The Institutional Review Board (IRB) was a legal requirement that had to be satisfied before the ELC could start. The IRB comprised an evaluation of the proposed research by a panel to ensure that all participants were protected from physical, psychological and sociological harm. Under IRB Category 11, it was determined that participants' involvement was ethical. A satisfactory IRB review signaled that the ELC could start.

A letter was sent requesting families' permission for their children to participate in the ELC by being video recorded in everyday classroom activities. Of the 100 families that were contacted each semester, approximately 95 families signed to give their permission. The children of families that declined were not included in video recordings or any other aspect of the ELC. Families did not participate in the professional development directly.

A Memorandum of Agreement (MOA) contract issued by the NYSOFCS itemized the roles and responsibilities of both the College and of each participating early childhood agency during each grant-funded semester. The College had to agree to meet grant goals, facilitate teachers' team leaders' and children's participation, communicate with families as necessary, communicate with NYSOFCS as stipulated, and manage the budget. Administrators and directors of Early Childhood agencies and settings were required to communicate with their executive boards and get participation clearance, give permission for video tapes of children to be recorded, provide a quiet room where professional development teams could meet each week for one hour to watch video recordings and reflect on their action research, support teams over the semester, provide substitute cover to release teachers from their teaching to enable them to attend professional development team meetings each week, oversee the budget and keep all grant materials for a statutory six year period. The MOA was agreed and signed by senior administrators at the College and by the senior administrator of each Early Childhood agency.

Directors of early childhood settings in which teacher candidates were placed for Practicum were each invited to participate in the ELC for one semester. If they accepted, they signed an agreement indicating that they would meet all grant requirements as determined by the College and by NYSOFCS. In addition, a sub-contract issued by the College Research Foundation set out the requirements and responsibilities that the Directors' governing board must agree to concerning: checking grant implementation in their Practicum classrooms, being familiar with ELC activity and responding to curriculum and teaching changes as they transpired.

The Theory of Action Research

Action Research has already been introduced in this book. Action Research was a professional development approach that was known to authors and so were confident to use it in the ELC. Definitions of Action Research illustrate why it was suited to the ELC. Cochran-Smith & Lytle, (1993) defined it as *research that educators do to investigate their own teaching in their own classrooms, to better understand and improve it.* Arhar, Meyers & Rust, (2003) said action research *contributes to the development of improved early childhood educational practice and theory.*

Other characteristics of Action Research that suited the ELC included promoting professional collaboration across different early childhood agencies, and, between different educators, teacher candidates and team leaders in Practicum settings. This collaboration had the potential to spread improved teaching practice further and support greater consistency between college methods courses and teaching practices in Practicum field placements (Karp, 2006). However, it must be acknowledged that collaboration among team members, who had not worked together before, could be risky, because it may require them to change their teaching, with uncertain outcomes for children in their own classrooms (Griffiths, 1990).

Another advantage of using Action Research in the ELC was that it was a democratic form of professional development that put teams in charge of their own professional development. The process did not impose prescriptive change on participants which they might resist (Fullen, 1993; Bainer & Wright, 2000). Instead, Action Research gave the teams choice and control over their professional decisions and actions. Teams developed skills that put the onus on them to improve their own teaching both now and in the future. Teams were encouraged to ask questions and explore their own values about teaching challenges they faced, that revealed their current levels of professional thinking and understanding (McNiff, Lomax & Whitehead, 2000).

The use of a constructivist approach in Action Research was helpful because it recognized that educators' teaching knowledge was built overtime and in layers of experience. New knowledge about new teaching practices in Action Research would then be built on prior knowledge and values about their teaching. A constructivist approach used in Action Research made it more likely that new teaching practices would be understood by teams and incorporated into their teaching (Kochan, 2000).

The problem-solving focus of Action Research accorded with the ELC because practical action and negotiated change were called for to address teaching challenges educators faced in their classrooms. When transformed into educators' new understanding about their teaching, problem-solving can improve practice and learning opportunities for team members and for children. More consistent practice in Practicum classrooms, that was more closely aligned with NAEYC standards at the college, could then be expected. (Karp, 2006, Helmsley-Brown and Sharp, 2003). However, Action Research has been criticized for its lack of rigor in comparison with scientific methods of educational research (Brause & Myer, 1993 p.133). A lack of replication beyond the classroom in which the Action Research was carried out was criticized by Dick (1993). However, the main aim of the ELC was not to create new educational knowledge to be tested, measured, compared across large-scale samples. Instead, it was to provide professional development opportunities to teams of educators in Practicum classrooms, to improve their knowledge and practice, concerning teaching challenges and closer alignment with NAEYC Standards (2009).

Training in the ELC

At the start of each semester, training workshops were provided by faculty at the college, to prepare team leaders, teacher candidates, directors and educators for the roles and responsibilities they faced in the ELC. Team leaders' roles and responsibilities. Training was undertaken at the start of the semester to prepare team leaders to guide and support teams in: using Action Research methods by using texts by Meyers & Rust, 2003, and Rust & Clark; following a weekly schedule to ensure project completion at the end of the semester; reading literature on the identified teaching problem and child development; selecting a strategy from the literature for implementation; creating an assessment tool to evaluate the implementation of the strategy; helping teacher candidates use video recorders and voice recorders to gather data; supporting the team in data analysis, reflection and formulating results. Each week throughout the semester, the team leader would lead hourly professional development team meetings that took place in the Practicum placement.

The roles and responsibilities of teacher candidates who agreed to participate in the professional development community. Teacher candidates attended a training workshop at the beginning of the semester and attended weekly professional development team meetings throughout the semester. Specifically, responsibilities of Practicum students were to: find professional literature that helped the team overcome a self-chosen teaching or care problem that was related to current NAEYC standards for initial teacher preparation; operate a video camera to record the implementation of a remedial strategy; operate a voice recorder to record weekly team meeting discussions; collaborate with the graduate student to embed iMovie video recording clips into a PowerPoint presentation; and lead the team presentation of their project at an end of semester conference.

Following each team's identification of their teaching or care problem, teacher candidates met with the college Teaching Materials Center librarian to search early childhood electronic databases for relevant journal articles that their teams could read. Journal articles published by NAEYC, that strongly reflected NAEYC Standards were copied and read by teams during team meetings. Journal articles were used to help teams learn more about their teaching or care problem, identify strategies to improve it, and, at the same time align teaching in Practicum classrooms with NAEYC standards.

A graduate assistant media technician based at the college provided training to teacher candidates on using video cameras, voice recorders and the construction of PowerPoint presentations in which iMovie clips were embedded. The presentations were shared with the local early childhood community at an end of semester professional development conference held at the college.

Each semester administrative duties comprised arranging and copying materials for training events for participants; arranging secure storage of grant materials (particularly video recordings of children in Practicum classrooms), downloading voice recordings onto a computer, filing documents related to participating teams and settings, checking video cameras and voice recorders worked properly, working with the media technician to support Practicum students in the construction of iMovie PowerPoint presentations.

The ELC training consisted of familiarizing team leaders, teacher candidates, directors and educators in using Action Research in their classrooms, by reading chapters from McNiff (2002) and by familiarizing them with each consecutive stage set out in Table 1.4 below. New stages added to the ELC Action Research model included teams at Stage (5) through Stage (8). The reading of professional literature was designed to establish the habit of teams consulting and using literature together. Through reading, teams new to Action Research were provided with early childhood professional knowledge that was concrete and was known to improve the teaching challenges they faced (Meyers & Rust, 2003; Dickinson, 2002). Reading deepened teams' knowledge about their teaching challenge and ensured their decision-making opportunities within Action Research. Abundant examples of early childhood educational research existed in journals, but fewer case studies illustrated how educators used reading to improve their teaching (Kochran, 2000, Nelson, Leffler, & Hansen, 2009).

Table 1.4: The ELC Action Research model

During Action Research, teams were introduced to two sources of literature that focused on the teaching challenge they identified. First, Using the NAEYC journal, *Young Children* was an obvious choice, because articles commonly reflected NAEYC Standards (2009), thereby modeling developmentally-appropriate practices, that had the potential to improve alignment between College class content and teaching practices in Practicum placements. Once teams had identified their teaching challenge, teacher candidates worked with the librarian at the College to carry out electronic database literature searches. Keywords connected to the teaching challenge were used to identify relevant journal articles at the website: https://www.naeyc.org/resources if relevant articles were not found in *Young Children*, other professional journals were available for searching e.g. *Early Childhood Education Journal* and *Early Childhood Research and Practice*.

Second, *Yardsticks* (Wood, 2007) was an informative reference book that enabled teams to check whether their chosen strategies in journals were developmentally-appropriate to implement with pre-school children in their Practicum placements. *Yardsticks* enabled teams to revise their understanding of typical pre-operational child development and the factors that affected it. For three-year-old pre-operational children not included in Yardsticks, other early childhood developmental texts were recommended, e.g., Wortham (2006); Allen & Marotz (2010).

Following identification and video recording of their teaching challenge, teams were prepared to critically read 3-4 relevant literature articles. Guided by the team leader, the team evaluated each article and then agreed on one strategy to implement in their placement. At the same time, teams referred to *Yardsticks* to evaluate the developmental appropriateness of the strategy, relative to the developmental stages and characteristics of the children in their class.

During each of four semesters, six participating teams followed a weekly calendar (see Table 1.5 below.) The calendar was designed to provide teams with clarity about weekly workflow and timely completion of their Action Research by the end of the semester.

Semester	Semester week number and week date	Date and time of team meeting	Activity	Location
Fall	Week 1, 8.18.	Mon 8.18. 3.00-4.30	Team leaders' induction and training	ACCC
	Week 2, 9.1.	Mon 9.1. 3.00-4.30	Complete IRB clearance	College
	Week 3, 9.8.	Thurs 9.8. 4.30-5.30	Directors, teachers Practicum students and team leaders' induction and training	College
	Week 4, 9.15.	Mon 9.15. 3.00-4.00	Identify the problem, video and view	Preschool setting
	Week 5, 9.22.	Mon 9.22. 3.00-4.00	Find literature on teaching problem and identify a strategy to implement	College library
	Week 6, 9.29.	Mon 9.29. 3.00-4.00	Plan, model, implement and record implementation of strategy.	Preschool setting
	Week 7, 10.6.	Mon 10.6. 3.00-4.00	Implement, record and reflect	Preschool setting
Mid grant payment	Week 8, 10.13.	Mon 10.13. 3.00-4.00	Implement, record and reflect	
	Week 9, 10.20.	Mon 10.20. 3.00-4.00	Implement, record and reflect	Preschool setting
	Week 10, 10.27.	Mon 10.27. 3.00-4.00	Implement, record and reflect	Preschool setting
	Week 11, 11.3.	Mon 11.3. 3.00-4.00	Analyze videos and identify findings	Preschool setting
	Week 12, 11.10.	Mon 11.10. 3.00-4.00	Reflect and prepare documentation panels	Preschool setting
	Week 13, 11.17.	Mon 11.17. 3.00-4.00	Reflect and prepare documentation panels	Preschool setting
	Week 14, 11.24.	Fall Break	Thanksgiving	College library
	Week 15, 12.1	Thurs 12.4. 2.30	Mini-conference presentations	College

Semester	Semester week number and week date	Date and time of team meeting	Activity	Location
		-5.00		
Final payment	Week 16, 12.8.	Mon 12.8. 3.00-4.00	Team leaders' final evaluation meeting	ACCC

Table 1.5. Weekly calendar for team activity over one semester

Data collection and analysis methods were used by teams to monitor the implementation of their strategy. Teams used mixed methods to collect and analyze data throughout their Action Research because both methods illuminated and complemented each other (Wellington, 2000). During weekly team meetings, data analysis enabled teams to quantify, evaluate and reflect on the impact of strategies on the teaching challenges they faced, on alignment with NAEYC Standards (2009), on educators' and teacher candidates' professional understanding and on children's learning (Bell, 1999). The data collection tools used during Action Research comprised: weekly report forms; video recordings; assessment checklists; voice recordings and, questionnaires. Team leaders completed the weekly report forms after each weekly team meeting. The purpose of weekly report forms was to: (1) indicate the action research work that teams were to undertake each week of the semester; (2) keep a weekly log of each team's progress in implementing the action research; (3) enable team leaders to identify and record findings during the action research; (4) assess how the team responded during weekly meetings throughout the semester and provide support as needed; and (5) use data recorded on weekly report forms in final State reports.

Team leaders analyzed the weekly report forms by searching for patterns, themes and repetitions that were relevant to the Action Research investigation. Team leaders used markers to color-code data into different categories. Categories were named to label common patterns identified during the implementation of the Action Research (Delamont, 1992). Categories were compared to reveal findings in the Action Research and illustrated how teams responded at each stage of implementation.

Video recordings were an efficient tool for teams to use to gather data in the ELC because they removed the burden to record events in writing and so reduced work load. Videos captured events in Practicum placements as they happened and enabled teams to watch them repeatedly. Teacher candidates used a mini-DV video camera and video tapes to record their team's implementation of one strategy over a semester. Although most teacher candidates were already proficient in using a mini-DV video camera, they underwent training to ensure they were competent in operating this technology. Teacher candidates used ethical actions in the videoing of young children in placements during Practicum.

Videos (each approximately 20 minutes long) were recorded by teacher candidates about 4-5 times over the semester. Recorded videos were stored by the graduate assistant who converted them into document files in readiness for analysis (Stemler, 2001). Teams watched videos at weekly team meetings to evaluate, analyze and reflect on: strategy implementation; impact on the teaching challenge, how teaching was affected; how children's learning was impacted and how far alignment with NAEYC Standards was achieved (Plowman, 1999; Heath & Hindmarsh, 2002; Walker, 2002; Walsh, 2007).

As teams watched each video recording, they used a checklist to consistently analyze it. (See Table 1.6 below: The strategy assessment checklist). Teams counted the frequency of outcomes observed in each video tape and compared the result from one tape to the next. Each week, teams answered the same questions about their

Action Research that enabled them to consistently evaluate and reflect on the impact of strategy implementation over the semester.

Strategy Assessment Checklist

The strategy assessment checklist is used when teams view videos of strategy implementation in their classrooms. Assessment criteria come from: (1) categories in the video data and (2) strategy outcomes identified by the team as illustrating effectiveness of the strategy. The assessment grid is used to record quantitative examples of the criteria in the frequency column and qualitative examples in the Comments column.

Practicum setting:

Date:

Video No:

Strategy:

Assessment Criteria	Frequency	Comments
Named categories:		
Strategy outcomes:		

Table 1.6: The strategy assessment checklist

Team reflection after video is viewed:

1. Is the strategy working? How?
2. Is the original teaching challenge being improved? How?
3. Is the children's learning improving? How?
4. Is your teaching changing? How?

5. Is your understanding of your teaching changing? How?

Team leaders used a digital voice recorder to record weekly team-meeting discussions. These were stored electronically by the graduate assistant on a laptop computer in a Wave voice format (WAV). Digital voice recorders were simple to use and left the team free to concentrate on discussion rather than writing down what was said (The National Centre for Technology in Education 2007). Each week teacher candidates returned the voice recorder, with saved voice files on it, to the team leader, who later analyzed Voice files qualitatively, by grouping recurring themes into named categories, concerning the impact of the strategy. At the end of each semester, analyzed data along with team discussions about video-tape data were used in the writing up of NYOFCS final reports.

At the end of each semester, questionnaires were given to the twelve participating educators in classrooms, and to the six participating teacher candidates, to gather their written evaluations of the Action Research professional development model. By this time, educators and teacher candidates had experienced a whole semester of Action Research professional development to reflect upon. Educators and teacher candidates were invited to anonymously write their responses because it gave them an opportunity to write freely.

Educators' questionnaires included both closed and open-ended questions that enabled both quantitative and qualitative analysis of data. Closed questions required them to check a Likert rating scale that asked them to identify how far they agreed or disagreed with a statement about the Action Research. These responses were analyzed quantitatively. Accompanying open-ended questions enabled educators to explain their ratings. The open-ended questions were analyzed qualitatively by looking for repetitions and patterns in their responses that were formed into categories and named (McNiff, Lomax and Whitehead, 1996). The questionnaire for teacher candidates comprised open-ended questions that required qualitative analysis using the same qualitative methods described for educators.

Presenting Findings

There is a responsibility among early childhood Action Researchers to disseminate the processes and results of their Action Research so that others may learn from it and improved teaching methods are used in policy documents and in classrooms (McNiff, Lomax & Whitehead, 2000, O'Hanlon 1994, Henderson 2004). Early childhood Action Research is often of a case-study design involving a small number of people working in one classroom. It is important that early childhood Action Researchers move beyond the confines of their own classrooms and become contributors to the early childhood field by showing others what they did and the impact it had on their own teaching development and on children's learning. When Action Researchers share their work at conferences and in workshops, they reach a larger audience. Action researchers can help other early childhood educators who face similar teaching and care problems to the ones they faced. They can demonstrate to administrators and faculty who work in different agencies, how theory and practice can work in harmony and help align Standards to promote greater consistency between theory and practice during Practicum for teacher candidates.

Early childhood educators and teacher candidates are commonly in the audience at early childhood conferences but less often do they make presentations together about their own Action Research carried out in their own classrooms (Nias, 1993). Early childhood educators and teacher candidates who have participated in Action Research together, have to be supported by more experienced supervisors and administrators, to go public about their professional development work, because of its authenticity. Reporting on the processes and results of early childhood Action Research that is located in classrooms with young children, provides the most compelling evidence of what works, and, what is therefore beneficial to future early childhood policy and practice. It also provides alternatives to present notions that early childhood professional development is about implementing Standards, without regard to important processes that support improved outcomes, and also, that purchased and even scripted programs imported into classrooms are the way to improve educators' practice.

The opportunity for ELC teams to disseminate their Action Research work took place at half-day conferences held at the college at the end of each semester. Six participating teams showed their 20 minute-long iMovie PowerPoint presentation to invited members of the local early childhood community that included New York State Office of Child and Family Services (NYSOCFS) officials, librarians, technical staff, faculty, Practicum directors and other Practicum students. About 60 delegates attended each conference. In addition, about three team leaders and teacher candidates showed their iMovie PowerPoint presentations at State early childhood conferences, to further spread the model at work. In addition, three team leaders presented their teams' Action Research work at national early childhood conferences.

Teacher candidates worked on their presentations throughout the semester of Action Research that included writing slides, editing and inserting video clips and voice recording clips and, reporting and reflecting on research results. At each end of semester conference, and with their teams present, teacher candidates led the presentation of their Action Research and answered questions from the audience. A rubric was used to evaluate teacher candidates' work and course credit duly awarded.

At the end of the grant implementation, IMovie PowerPoint presentations were organized into a database of DVDs. These were used in subsequent early childhood college methods classes to model consistency of NAEYC Standards based college methods course content and teaching in Practicum placements. In addition, databases illustrated changed teaching among educators that resulted in improved learning opportunities for both teacher candidates and children. Final case-study reports of Action Research work undertaken at each participating Practicum setting and its results were submitted to NYSOCFS at the end of each semester. These reports constituted a permanent record of the ELC at work.

In Part II of this book, six ELC case studies of early childhood professional development are presented showing what teams of educators did to improve the teaching challenges they faced in their classrooms. Each case study show how teams used our ELC Action Research model to investigate teaching challenges in their classrooms; aligned new teaching practices more closely with NAEYC early childhood professional standards for initial teacher preparation; and reported on the responses of participants to the ELC. The six case studies were selected for inclusion in this book because they represented the same teaching challenges reported by teacher candidates, concerning: children's poor quality free play; few opportunities for children to explore concepts in content areas; the problematical behavior of young boys; and, a lack of effective inclusion of each child with diverse learning needs.

To help readers, a summary of the Action Research carried out in each case study is provided at the start of each chapter.

PART II: CASE STUDIES

2. IMPROVING CHILDREN'S SOCIO-DRAMATIC PLAY

What is "socio-dramatic play?" It is the mechanism in which children recreate, through their natural inclination to play, incidents they have experienced and/or have made up in fantasy.

Teaching Challenge

Children's socio-dramatic play was deemed inadequate.

Background

Strategy: The approach was to introduce "talking time" during the circle time, when the children would come together as a group and activities were planned for the day. This served "Talking Time" to create opportunities for children to express ideas for socio-dramatic play, and to generate ways for educators to support those ideas.

Context: The action research took place in a rural Head-Start Pre-K classroom for 4-5 year olds. There were 16 children in the class with a lead educator and an assistant educator. Full day care was provided to children including those with exceptional learning needs. Educators used the High/Scope curriculum and Head-Start learning outcomes to guide their teaching.

Summary

The introduction of a strategy called "Talking Time" to Circle time gave children a daily opportunity to express their own ideas for socio-dramatic play and how educators should support their play. Once educators understood children's ideas, they knew how to progressively facilitate the socio-dramatic play through relevant conversations, provision of appropriate play materials, and intentionally including children into the play. Video recordings enabled educators to track individual children's involvement in the development of the play.

Findings

(1) Children's fleeting socio-dramatic play existed, but educators did not recognize it.

(2) Children's imaginative play was only apparent when educators asked them "open-ended" questions. An open-ended question requires more than a 'yes' or 'no' answer.

(3) "Talking Time" revealed that boys often had multiple, dynamic, and sequential ideas for socio-dramatic play.

(4) Children's ideas comprised fantasy and real topics and often included moral themes.

(5) Children had creative ideas about how they could use materials to make their own play props.

(6) Children's ideas for socio-dramatic play moved between circle time, the art area, and the socio-dramatic center.

(7) When children shared props, their play was more inclusive and encouraged control over their own actions.

(8) When children used their own ideas in socio-dramatic play, educators observed their greater use of literacy and mathematical skills and educators were able to transition to facilitating rather than controlling the play.

Educators identified the poor quality of children's socio-dramatic play in this challenge, and described it thus: Few children went into the socio-dramatic play area, and if they did, they did not stay there for any significant amount of time. Children's play was thought to be "basic" because they commonly used objects in literal ways, e.g., a child holds a doll and offers it a drink from a cup, as seen in fig. 2.1. Educators wondered if computer games had robbed children of imagination. Children, the educators speculated, were now used to being entertained, and were far less inclined to make up their own play plots or sustain them. Working parents had little time to interact and play with their children which may be one explanation for the lack of children's socio-dramatic play.

Fig. 2.1: The teaching challenge ~ children's socio-dramatic play was inadequate

To investigate the challenge further, the teacher candidate recorded a video of the children in the socio-dramatic play area. As educators watched the video, they more fully comprehended and described the teaching challenge, and expressed their own beliefs about socio-dramatic play.

Many children, boys in particular, did not interact in the socio-dramatic play area. Some boys were disruptive and broke each other's props. Boys tended to act out roles on their own, e.g., changing the baby and mopping the floor. Educators said the boys did not play well together. Socio-dramatic play had a "cookie-cutter" quality about it and was described as "boring." Educators wondered how they could get children, and boys in particular, to interact more in the socio-dramatic area. Sustaining the play was also part of the challenge because it often consisted of isolated tasks that were gender traditional and difficult to develop, e.g., carrying the baby around and changing the baby's diaper.

Materials in the socio-dramatic area reflected everyday situations, e.g., going to a restaurant or visiting a beauty shop. Children used cooking pots and dress-up clothes, but materials were not used imaginatively to represent other purposes. The lack of imaginative plots made further development of the play more difficult.

Values about Socio-Dramatic Play

Educators said socio-dramatic play supported children's development, both social and emotional. It helped children accept others who were different from themselves, and to learn tolerance of children with diverse needs. The socio-dramatic area offered boys the opportunity to take on roles that challenged stereotypical male behavior. It was thought useful for boys to act out traditionally female roles because they could then learn about social and family dynamics of varied composition.

Alignment with NAEYC Standards

The value of play in children's lives was emphasized in NAEYC Standards (2009) and was articulated in detail in Standard 1: Promoting Child Development and Learning; Standard 3: Observing, Documenting and Assessing to Support Young Children and Families; and Standard 4: Using Developmentally Effective Approaches to Connect with Children and Families. Well prepared early childhood teacher candidates were required to base their practice on a sound knowledge and understanding of young children's characteristics and needs through play. They were to provide children with opportunities to play and learn so that they understood and made sense of experiences both through spontaneous and guided investigations. Because spontaneous play was a powerful force in support of children's development, well-prepared teacher candidates were expected to observe and support children in playful situations and in more formal learning contexts.

Aims of the Action Research

The aims of this action research project were to enable the team to improve socio-dramatic play, aligning it with relevant standards; building consistency for teacher candidates between their college and Practicum experiences; and, improving teacher candidates' planning and teaching of their socio-dramatic play lesson.

Creating a Baseline Assessment

The team created a "check-list" of the teaching challenges they identified. While watching a 20-minute video of children in the socio-dramatic area, the team was able to count the frequency of each behavior to assess how problematic it was.

Teaching Challenges in socio-dramatic play	Frequencies
Children do not play together	6
Children do not share materials	3
Socio-dramatic play is mundane	5
Socio-dramatic play is not sustained	3
Socio-dramatic play area is underused	3
Socio-dramatic play is stereo-typical	1
Socio-dramatic play is not imaginative	4
Pretend play not evident	2
Children's own ideas lacking	3
Socio-dramatic play is static	3
Children do not self-regulate	4

Table 2.1: The checklist of teaching challenges in socio-dramatic play

Thirty-seven behaviors were recorded in categories of challenge. Six examples of solitary or parallel play indicated that children seldom played together. Children copied one another as they carried dolls around and fed them. Children commented, "I'm sitting next to my baby," and "I'm a dad." On four occasions, children played with materials in literal ways, e.g., holding a bottle to the baby's mouth. Children did not often share materials. On five occasions, the team described the play as "mundane" because children did not speak or develop the play beyond repetitive actions. The play was uninspiring for the team, if not necessarily for the children. On four occasions, play was not sustained. The socio-dramatic area was underused because only seven out of 16 children played there over the 20-minute period. Single gender play was not often stereotypical. All children, regardless of whether they were a boy or a girl, largely played out domestic roles. On five occasions, children played parental roles that appeared to be in response to the play materials at hand. On three occasions, the play was static because it did not develop beyond the use of materials in literal ways. For example, babies were put in high chairs at feeding times, and cups were used to give babies drinks. One boy said while mopping the floor, "I'm making it nice and clean."

Only one example of self-regulation was observed when a child attempted to solve a problem. The child wanted to feed his baby with a bottle, and offered another child a cup in exchange for the bottle she was using. As educators watched the video, and recorded the frequencies of challenges, they reflected that they would have expected children in the 4 to 5-year old age range to demonstrate higher levels of play. The team was concerned that the children who had been in the classroom for one semester already had not yet formed friendships necessary to engage in social play. However, several children with special needs played alone so the diversity of ability had to be taken into account.

The team noticed other unexpected but positive behaviors in the video. A child who rarely played in the socio-dramatic area spent a prolonged period changing a baby's diaper. A girl, described as a "flitter," spent considerable time making a chain out of links which required a definite level of concentration. Educators observed in footage toward the end of the video, six fleeting examples of pretend play concerned with dragons. A quiet child was identified as having initiated the dragon play. Educators were shocked that this child had such imaginative ideas for pretend play about dragons, even as the children were seen hiding in cupboards and wearing hats to represent themselves as dragons.

Had the children not been recorded, the educators would never have seen these fleeting instances of play. One teacher said, "I had no idea how they started playing dragons. I didn't know so much went on. We really need to sit down and pay attention to the play. What did it mean when they put bowls on their heads to represent being dragons?"

Educators had recorded observations of children on a daily basis, however, as a means to provide evidence of specific Head Start learning outcomes, behaviors *not* included were not recorded. After discovering that they had undoubtedly missed these instances of play, the team wanted to find ways to improve their ability to identify and record such behaviors in the future.

Developing Dragon Play

The team decided to act immediately to sustain the dragon play before it disappeared. Educators realized that because they had not seen the dragon play before, their evaluation of children's learning and development was inaccurate. The team showed the video to the children the next day and asked them to explain what was happening. Children were asked open-ended questions to support the dragon play, e.g., "What can we do to help you play? What can I bring for you?"

Results

At the next team meeting, educators reported that children were full of "great ideas that showed their thinking in their fantasy play." Children's answers to questions revealed how they were aware of "evil versus good forces." Some children said they were either "good" or "bad" dragons. Children described their roles in the play. Even though the dragons were invisible, children hid in holes with them. Children identified the materials they needed to develop their play, e.g., costumes to act out the role of princesses, paper shields to protect them from the dragons' fire, dragons' wings to fly and a reindeer nose. Children planned to build a dragon's den with a roof, walls, and a door with handles so they could lock the "bad" dragon out.

Team Reflection

Educators reflected on how asking questions had improved their ability to learn about children's play. Previously they were not aware of the content of children's play, or, of how they could support it. As a result, educators underestimated children's social, intellectual, and creative abilities. Children used three areas of the classroom at the same time. During circle time, the whole group of 16 children discussed plans for socio-dramatic play. In the art area, ten children made props for the play. In the socio-dramatic play area, six children played out the plot. Educators described how children demonstrated more self-regulation as all abilities worked cooperatively, acted out their own ideas, organized the play, made props, problem-solved, and developed the plot from day to day. Educators remarked how they themselves really enjoyed the play and wanted to know how to sustain it.

Selected Literature

The teacher candidate worked with the college librarian and found three journal articles for the team to read:

(1) Egan, K. (1991) Young children's imagination and learning: Engaging children's emotional response. *Young Children* 49 (6) 27-32.

(2) Howell, J. & Corbey-Scullen, L. (1997) Out of the socio-dramatic keeping corner and onto the stage – extending dramatic play. *Young Children* 52(6) 82-88.

(3) Manz, D. (1966) This is the socio-dramatic area that Kindergarten built. *Young Children* 52 (1).

The team chose one strategy from the article *Out of the Socio-dramatic keeping corner and Onto the Stage – Extending Dramatic Play*. The strategy called *"Talking Time"* gave children opportunities to express their ideas for socio-dramatic play and explain how the educators could support those ideas (Howell & Corbey-Scullen, (1997) p 83). The strategy reinforced what educators had already started doing during circle time.

The team also referred to Wood (2007) to confirm that the talking time strategy was developmentally appropriate for 4 to 5-year-old children.

Assessment of the Strategy

The team developed a second checklist...*a strategy assessment grid* (see completed version at Table 2.2) to assess and measure the effectiveness of the "Talking Time" strategy. They identified desirable socio-dramatic play outcomes to help them know what to look for in videos, and to determine what constituted evidence of improvement. Questions were devised to guide the team's consistent reflection. The strategy assessment grid was used each time the team viewed a video.

First Stage of Strategy Implementation

Fig. 2.2: Implementing the "talking time" strategy

A 20-minute video showed the first stage of the "talking time strategy" during circle time. Analysis of the video revealed the following.

Assessment Criteria	Frequency	Comments
*Children suggest characters	6	Roles in play
*Children suggest educators' roles	1	To provide materials
*Children express ideas for play	34	Boys contribute fully
*Plot is dynamic	4	Different plots suggested
*Children resolve own problems (self-regulate)	21	Rationale for thinking
Boys interact in play		
Boys share materials		
Use materials creatively		
Play is novel		New scenarios are suggested

Assessment Criteria	Frequency	Comments
Play area is well used (how many children?)		
Play is inclusive		
*Play plot is imaginative		Very imaginative
*Pretend play exists		Frequently
*Children go in and out of role		Long enough to explain play
* Assessed during "talking time" at circle time		

Table 2.2: Video analysis checklist

Team reflection after video is viewed:

- Is the strategy working? How?
- Is the original teaching challenge being improved upon? How?
- Is children's learning improving? –How?
- Is your understanding of your teaching changing? How?
- Is your teaching changing? How?

Video Analysis and Results

One week after the introduction of "talking time," the teacher candidate recorded a video during circle time. Using the strategy assessment grid at Table 2.3, analysis showed that children suggested character roles on six occasions in different play plots. Plots included: a man to pay for puppies bought in the pet store; a person to take dogs outside; a pet doctor; a fishing pole maker, and a team of good dragons. The talking time strategy was highly effective in providing educators with opportunities to ask children to come up with their own ideas about characters and roles in socio-dramatic play.

Children asked educators to provide them with materials to make props for the play. On 34 occasions children requested paper to make signs to keep dragons out of the play area, an X-ray machine for the veterinarian, flames for the dragons, tape and string to make spiders' webs, a syringe to vaccinate pets; a fish tank, a fishing pole, and a rope.

Children suggested four play plots that included: a pet store called "Animal Actions;" the dragon's den; a fishing trip and spiders which indicated that children held multiple play-plots in their minds at one time. Play plots were dynamic and included ones they had performed before. The teaching challenge of static play was overcome. Children showed 21 examples of resolving their own problems with props in the play. This included explaining why certain materials were needed in the pet store. For example, a table was needed "so dogs could lie down" and another table was needed to help "dogs with an infection." In response to the teacher's question about why they should get an X-ray machine, one child responded, "We could buy it so we could look at bones." Children suggested making "spider webs, tall bridges, and a door with a lock on it," as suitable deterrents to keep the bad dragons out of the socio-dramatic area.

Fig. 2.3: The impact of talking time on children's socio-dramatic play

Boys dominated "talking time" discussions and contributed many new imaginative ideas for pretend play. One boy said "We need to work as a team to keep mean dragons out." Boys slipped in and out of pretend roles as they described play-plots and materials educators could provide to make props. This result suggested that Talking Time provided the children, and boys in particular, with opportunities to express highly imaginative play ideas that the educators needed to listen to.

Team Reflections

Questions on the strategy assessment grid at table 2.3 guided team reflection. "Talking Time" worked well as it allowed educators, including the teacher candidate, to create daily opportunities for children's ideas to be expressed during circle time. The team concluded that the teaching challenges concerning children's mundane play, in which their own imaginative ideas did not feature, were overcome.

With more imaginative play, many aspects of the original teaching challenge were improved. A teacher commented, "There has been a blossoming of children's ideas that are key to improving socio-dramatic play."

Children's learning improved in many ways. Wider vocabulary was used as children participated in planning discussions and then in acting out the play. Children's literacy skills were reinforced when they saw educators write their ideas for plans on a flip chart. Children "wrote" letters and numbers as they created props. They expressed their creativity as they made props for their play. During free-play time, educators commented how the whole curriculum rotated between circle time, the art area, and the socio-dramatic play area.

Educators' understanding of their teaching techniques changed. Initially, educators had set up the socio-dramatic area, but now they asked the children questions about the area, and listened to their answers. Educators learned how to successfully support and sustain the play. Educators commented that the video had been an invaluable tool in helping them see the impact of talking time on children's learning. Watching it several times helped to make sense of what was happening.

Educators said their own teaching had changed because they had a better understanding of children's thinking. Changes in educators' roles and practices were identified. Educators were much more involved with listening to children's play ideas and helping children fabricate the resources they would need to act out them out. Educators said they enjoyed observing the children's play more now, because it was so much richer than before. The way in which children used multiple classroom play areas meant educators were able to participate in the planning, resourcing, and acting out of the play. One teacher described the change in her teaching as "an explosion, but in a really, really good way."

The strategy provided opportunities for NAEYC standards 1, 3 and 4 to be met. Requirements concerning educators improved the following: understanding of young children's development and learning through fantasy play; increasing children's reasoning and understanding through play; and providing opportunities to observe and support children's play. These improvements were now featured during Practicum. The teacher candidate experienced improved consistency between the content she learned in college courses and professional practice during Practicum.

Second Stage of Implementation of the Strategy

A second 20-minute video was recorded to discover the impact of the strategy on the quality of children's learning during socio-dramatic play. The following criteria and frequencies were observed and recorded:

Assessment Criteria	Frequency	Comments
Children suggest characters	0	
Children suggest educators' roles	0	
Children express ideas for play	0	
Plot is dynamic	0	
Children resolve own problems (self-regulate)	0	
* Boys interact in play	10	Dragon flight, signs
* Boys share materials	3	Bandages, doctor's kit
* Use materials creatively	8	Signs, shots, syringe, stop sign
* Play is novel	3	Copies Christmas list, numbers
* Play area is well used (how many children?)	8	Changing, doctors, dragons, vets
* Play is inclusive	3	Door to let in or out
* Play is imaginative	6	Boys with dragon claws, shields
* Pretend play exists	7	Dragons, binding pet's tail
* Children go in and out of role	3	Stop signs
* Assessed during socio-dramatic play		

Table 2.3: The strategy's impact on children's learning during socio-dramatic play

Boys interacted with other boys on ten occasions. They lay on the floor acting out the roles of knights and dragons. Some flapped their wings and roared like dragons. Others held shields up to protect their eyes. Boys searched for the dragon that slept under the table saying, "Don't wake him up!" Two boys gave "bad dragons" shots to make them better. Boys stuck "written" signs on the den. They shared materials on three occasions... when they used the doctor's kit on sick animals; bandaged a sick cat's tail; and gave animals shots. Boys mended a broken shield by applying new tape to the back. On two occasions, boys held the trains of girls dressed as princesses, and the pairs processed up and down the classroom. The quality of socio-dramatic play was greatly enhanced by children's increased opportunities to plan and discuss their own imaginative play plots, to move around freely to develop the play, to solve problems, to manipulate materials and to use literacy and mathematical skills. As a result, the challenges of children not playing together, not showing imagination, and not sharing materials were greatly reduced.

Fig. 2.4: Children interact and make props for socio-dramatic play

Children used materials creatively in the art area on eight occasions. They "wrote" signs to put at the entrance to the den. One boy made a syringe to treat sick dragons and represented the liquid with a strand of wool. Many children made pairs of symmetrically decorated wings. Girls made crowns to go with their princess dresses. One child made antlers, a tail, and a pink nose to wear so she could represent "Rudolph the Red-Nosed Reindeer." Another child made a paper lock to keep bad dragons out. Evidence suggested that the teaching challenge concerning a lack of pretend play was conquered.

The play incorporated surprising elements of ingenuity on three occasions. One child used a list of children's names displayed on the classroom wall to copy letters onto a sign. Children wrote numbers on signs and placed them at the entrance to the socio-dramatic area. Up to eight children were seen in the socio-dramatic area at one time. The play spilled over into art and literacy areas of the room so that, at times, all 16 children in the class were involved. Much of the play focused on concepts of dragons being "good or bad" and "in or out" of the socio-dramatic area, suggesting that children had their own ways of exploring moral concepts. Evidence showed that challenges concerning the previously underused, stereo-typical, socio-dramatic play area were solved.

On six occasions children took on pretend roles, moved between classroom areas, and played in three play-plots at one time. Children acted out pretend roles as they fanned dragons' flames, played Mr. Wolf, and imagined the dragons either inside or outside of the socio-dramatic area. Children moved easily in and out of roles as they either played a role, or gave instructions that were relevant to the role. For example, one child said, "The dragons want to come in." Another responded: "Get a door knob (to lock them out). A third said, "She's making the doorknob out of paper." This evidence suggested that the play was highly imaginative and that children thought and communicated on multiple levels during the socio-dramatic play. The teaching challenge concerned with dull, unimaginative, and mundane play was overcome.

Team Reflections

The "talking time" strategy was very successful. When children were able to initiate their own ideas for play, new opportunities were created for educators to "jump right in and support their learning and development."

The team was pleasantly surprised at the overlap between play plots. The play moved quickly between wolves, the zoo, coyotes, fishing, and dragons. By using the rug, art, block and socio-dramatic areas, children's play was expanded beyond the socio-dramatic area throughout the classroom.

Children's learning was definitely improving. When making props, children developed new literacy skills by using sentence strips to read and write signs. In play, children creatively used materials to represent objects they needed. They showed their understanding of concepts and knowledge across curriculum areas. One teacher commented: "How would we have ever known that shields were made to protect their faces from the dragons' fire?"

Educators' understanding of their teaching was changing. They abandoned their belief that socio-dramatic play only took place in the area designated for that purpose. They no longer believed that play was focused on one play plot at a time. Educators no longer thought that children's play was based on real-life events. Instead they were surprised to see children's interest in moral ideas such as *good* forces being allowed "in" and *bad* forces being kept "out." Educators described an example of this behavior when a child used a fishing pole to "catch" a bad wolf. He took the wolf out of the socio-dramatic area, placed him in a cage, and locked him up in a zoo.

Teaching roles in the classroom changed. Educators and teacher candidates' practice was improved during Practicum. They were amazed at children's play that showed examples of leadership, tolerance, and concern for what the children identified as "good" and "bad" forces. Educators no longer took on a supervisory role during play. During circle time each day, they carefully listened to the children's ideas. Educators observed children's socialization that indicated who led, who followed, who was an outsider, and what friendship groups existed in the classroom. The talking time strategy enabled teams' practice to be aligned with NAEYC standards 1, 3 and 4.

Third Stage of Strategy Implementation: Educators' Roles in Socio-Dramatic Play

Developing the roles educators played in socio-dramatic play required further improvement. The talking time strategy successfully allowed educators to take on new roles. They were better able to hear and understand play ideas and provide new materials for children to make props to act out their ideas. However, educators also wanted to discover and quantify the effect of their involvement in socio-dramatic play. A final video showed their impact and was logged on the assessment criteria grid:

Assessment Criteria	Frequency	Comments
Children suggest characters	0	
Children suggest educators' roles	0	
Children express ideas for play	0	
Plot is dynamic	0	
Children resolve own problems (self-regulate)	0	
* Boys interact in play	4	
* Boys share materials	4	
* Use materials creatively	5	
* Play is novel	5	Many play plots developed
* Play area is well used (how many children?)	5	
* Play is inclusive	6	Large groups involved in play
* Play is imaginative	5	Fantasy play
* Pretend play exists	5	Throughout the play
* Children go in and out of role	2	As they give instructions
* Assessed during socio-dramatic play		

Table 2.4: Educators' involvement in socio-dramatic play

One educator and four children hid from wolves by covering their heads with blankets. Children howled like wolves and ducked to the ground to avoid a lion. One child asked while pointing to a hiding place on the floor, "Are they still in there?" The teacher sat with a crown on her head and pretended to be a wolf. A second child asked, "Are they still there?" Children jumped as they moved the blankets down from their faces to peep and check whether the wolves were still in the hiding place. One child, who was a lead player, narrated what happened throughout the play.

Team Reflections

The team reported that the "Talking Time" strategy had worked "wonderfully" because it gave educators access to children's ideas for play. When educators understood these ideas, they were in an informed position to support play effectively.

The quality of socio-dramatic play had improved beyond all expectations. Educators could see the different content areas and associated concepts embedded in those areas. They commented how concepts, for example, concerned with "putting locks on doors to keep bad dragons out" would never have occurred to them. Using syringes to give puppies injections to make them well was beyond educators' own imagination.

Children's learning was much improved. Their fantasy play removed learning from the confines of mundane everyday situations, with outcomes addressing all content areas. Concepts in the content areas were wider and more elaborate than educators had expected.

Educators' understanding of their teaching changed from their being directors to facilitators of socio-dramatic play. They increasingly understood more about young children's thought and how it differed from their own. Even when children answered questions at circle time, it was not always easy for educators to respond appropriately. Children's thinking, they found, was qualitatively different from their own. Educators were learning to enter the play, and to respond to children through play.

Three themes emerged concerning the educators' new teaching roles. First, close proximity to children was important for educators' understanding of the play. When educators participated, they could see the socialization patterns among children, i.e., who developed, who followed, and who was on the margins of the play.

The second theme concerned educators' fear of overly directing the play. To avoid this, educators asked children for their opinions, and required explanations of what was happening. Educators asked leading questions, for example, "How far does the awning need to be lowered for the pit-crew?' and "Tell us why the wolves came?" Educators reflected on the origin of children's ideas and wondered where they had gotten their information about wolves and zoos. Children's ability to generate imaginative thoughts was more apparent to the educators when they participated in the play. When educators observed, interacted and conversed with children at the art table, they recognized inventiveness of children.

Third, involvement in the play helped educators assess children's abilities more accurately. Closer observation revealed children's ideas and resourcefulness.

Final Reflections

The aims of the action research were achieved. Reading about and implementing the "Talking Time" strategy had a transformative effect on educators' teaching. Improved early childhood teaching practices resulted in closer alignment with NAEYC Standards (2009) 1, 2 and 3. By the end of the semester, elements of Standard 4: Using Developmentally Effective Approaches to Connect with Children and Standard 5: Using Content Knowledge to Build Meaningful Curriculum were also met. "Talking Time" nurtured positive relationships between educators and children. Children's learning was evident in content areas including language and literacy, the arts, science and social studies. Greater consistency existed between the theory taught in college classes and educators' practice in classrooms. The teacher candidate's understanding of how high quality socio-dramatic play looked in action helped her write her lesson plan assignments.

The original teaching challenge was much improved through talking time. Time was allotted and opportunities were created each day for educators to listen and respond appropriately to children's ideas. Children articulated their imaginative ideas and learned through the applied play experiences. Once educators relinquished control of the play, they no longer set up the play scenarios, but instead responded to what children told them. As a result, children's learning improved in social, physical, language, intellectual, creative and emotional developmental areas. The use of video cameras during talking time improved educators' assessment. Educators saw and observed the entire play and did not merely look for predetermined learning outcomes. Educators valued children's play more highly and no longer missed children's ideas expressed in fantasy. More accurate assessments were carried out and that meant children's abilities were no longer underestimated.

Talking time changed educators' values about socio-dramatic play. Educators worked to change their adult perceptions, and instead appreciated children's fantasy-based ideas. "Talking time" enabled educators to re-evaluate the role of *parents* in children's socio-dramatic play as well. Busy parents, they concluded, did not have to be barriers to children's imaginative play. Instead, families were encouraged to observe and participate in it at home because of the rich learning opportunities that imaginative play presented. At the start of the action research, educators identified the teaching challenge as "boys' *lack* of imaginative play." Talking time had amazed educators by revealing that boys had a wealth of ideas for play and were often the play leaders in the classroom. Educators next decided to focus on the needs of girls in socio-dramatic play.

3. DEVELOPING A SCIENCE AREA

Teaching Challenge

Lack of a well-developed science area in a Pre-K classroom.

Background

Strategy: Creating a designated science area to improve children's scientific learning.

Context: The action research took place over one semester in a rural Head-Start pre-kindergarten classroom for 4-5 year olds. Full daycare was provided to children of all abilities including those with exceptional learning needs. There were 16 children in the class with a teacher and an assistant teacher. The High/Scope curriculum was used in the classroom.

Findings

1. The number of observed science learning indicators demonstrated by children increased from 16 to 74.
2. The number of science categories in which science indicators were observed increased from three to six.
3. A designated science area in the classroom resulted in educators giving science a higher priority in the curriculum.
4. Multiple examples of the same materials increased children's exploration.
5. Children most frequently used their senses of sight and touch to explore science materials.
6. Children engaged most with materials they could manipulate.

7. The presence of an adult in the science area resulted in children staying in the area for longer periods of time, using more language, and socializing more.
8. Literacy and math concepts in the science area needed to be purposefully supported by adults.
9. Time and materials needed to be made available to children in the science area for them to record their science observations.
10. Science concepts that children explored in the science area were extended during adult-guided small group activities.

Summary of the Action Research

The aim was to create an area specifically designed to improve children's scientific learning. Providing children with adequate time and materials to explore in the science area resulted in increased instances of science learning and use of scientific language; increased use of senses; and increased socialization. Educators more effectively supported children's active learning in the science area, and gave science a higher priority in the curriculum. Children spent more time in the science area, and their science learning was extended into directed small group and whole group times. A speech therapist used the science area to support a child with language delay. This was a change from taking him out of the classroom for speech therapy.

The Teaching Challenge

The teaching challenge was presented as a lack of a well-developed science area to support children's learning in that discipline.

Four reasons existed to explain this challenge. First, access to appropriate science materials was limited, but the team knew that children could still use everyday materials to explore science concepts, e.g., manipulating nuts and bolts with their hands to explore shape. The use of portable science kits provided one solution but the circulation between several Head-Start settings made consistent availability a problem.

Second, the emphasis on literacy in the Head-Start curriculum resulted in the neglect of science provision. At the time of the challenge, science provision was sporadic at best, but the team wanted to feature it in the curriculum on a daily basis to stimulate the children's scientific curiosity.

Third, educators' confidence in their own ability to teach science was problematic. Educators favored more science in the curriculum, and they wanted it to be fun for children, but they were not confident that their own knowledge of biology, physics, and chemistry would enable them to do this. And lastly, children were rarely drawn to the existing science area or the materials in it.

Fig 3.1: The teaching challenge ~ children's play is undeveloped in the science area

Team Values

The team highly valued science in the preschool curriculum. Science provided children with opportunities to explore concepts, investigate materials, and develop a sense of wonder about the world around them. Science provision was strong during adult-directed small-group times, e.g., making play-dough, hatching chicks, growing pumpkins, and cooking spaghetti, but science was not well resourced as a free-choice. Educators believed that scientific concepts and materials should be made freely available to children to build their literacy, mathematics and problem-solving skills.

Aim of the Action Research

The aim of this action research was to: (1) create a well-resourced science area that would support each child's scientific exploration and learning; (2) enable all children to have access to the science area during free-play times on a daily basis; (3) align science provision with NAEYC Standards (2009); (4) provide teacher candidates with a Practicum field experience in which these standards—and college course content regarding the teaching of science—was consistent; and (5) improve teacher candidates' opportunities to plan and implement science assignments during Practicum that reflected NAEYC Standards (2009).

Alignment with NAEYC Standards (2009)

The importance of teaching content in the early childhood curriculum is emphasized in NAEYC Standard 5: Using Content Knowledge to Build Meaningful Curriculum. Teacher candidates are required to use academic disciplines to design, implement, and evaluate experiences that promote security and regulation, problem solving and thinking, and academic competence in every young child. Teacher candidates are required to further support their science teaching and children's science learning by identifying and using developmentally appropriate practices and resources that include books, standards, documents, web resources, and to utilize individuals who have specialized content expertise.

Baseline Assessment

A 20-minute long video was recorded to form a baseline assessment of how children used science materials during free-choice time, a component of the High/Scope curriculum. Four girls played in a newly designated science area of the classroom. The team chose to use the Head Start Child Outcomes Framework for Science to analyze the video (see below Table 3.1), as it corresponded with their curriculum requirements. The video was analyzed for the frequency of observed science indicators.

Indicators	Frequencies
Use senses and a variety of tools and simple measuring devices to gather information, investigate materials and observe processes and relationships	10
Observe and discuss common properties, differences and comparisons among objects and materials	3
Participate in investigations to test observations, discuss and draw conclusions and form generalizations	0
Collect, describe, and record information through discussion, drawings, maps and charts	0
Make predictions, explanations and generalizations based on past experiences	0
Observe, describe, and discuss the natural world, materials, living things and natural processes	0
Know about and respect their bodies and the environment	0
Know ideas and use language related to time and temperature	0
Know about changes in materials and cause-effect relationships	3

Table 3.1: Frequency of Head Start Child Outcomes Framework for Science

Data Analysis and Team Reflection

16 science indicators were recorded on the video. As children investigated the geo-boards, feely boxes, and colored lenses, they used their senses of sight, hearing, language and touch. Children mostly played in parallel as they manipulated rubber bands and stretched them over geo-boards. A child asked another, "What are you doing?" and the other child replied, "I'm playing with the feely box." The child peered into the feely box, felt objects, and matched them to a corresponding picture card, e.g., the child matched a puppet with a picture card of a puppet.

The team identified three main themes about their science provision. First, the new science area gave science a higher priority in the curriculum than before. The new area occupied a better position than the previous science shelves. However, the space was not fully utilized. The new science area was not yet attractive to children, and a abscene of recorded frequencies for many of the indicators suggested that a full-range of scientific outcomes for children was not yet evident.

Second, children explored materials in the ways educators had hoped they would. The geo-boards with rubber bands, magnifying boxes, colored lenses, and feely box with matching cards all provided children with opportunities for sensory and manipulative exploration. However, the team agreed that science provision was weak in the curriculum, and questioned what science content children learned through such free-play activities. The team wondered if children had had experiences at home that provided them with prior knowledge or curiosity about scientific concepts. The team questioned what the children understood about concepts they had been exposed to.

Third, the results of the baseline assessment prompted the team to improve the science area. Plans were aimed at providing children with a broad range of materials that supported their learning in all areas of science. Educators aimed to use teaching strategies that supported children's active learning through free-choice, initiative, investigation, persistence, understanding cause and effect, and predicting outcomes.

Selected Literature

The teacher candidate worked with the college librarian to identify key words to search for journal articles that would help the team improve their teaching challenge. The following articles published in *Young Children* were found and read by the team:

(1) Hoisington, C. (2002). Using photographs to support children's science inquiry. *Young Children* 57 (5): 26-32.

(2) Jones, J., & Courtney, R. (2002). Documenting early science learning. *Young Children* 57 (5): 34-40.

(3) Buchanan, B.L., &. Rios, J.M. (2004). Teaching science to kindergartners: How can educators implement science standards? *Young Children* 59 (3): 82-87.

(4) Ross, M.E. (2000). Science their way. *Young Children* 55 (2): 6-13.

The article, "Science their way," was selected by the team because a strategy outlined in the article to create "*explorer kits*" appealed to them. The strategy consisted of gathering and organizing science materials, tools, and science-themed literature into kits. The strategy reinforced the team's goals of wanting children to learn science through manipulation of materials, open-ended inquiry and the use of literature to support content learning during free-play times. The role of the educator described in the article was appealing. It required that educators not teach science directly to children, but to facilitate science learning by providing children with time, space, equipment and literature. Educators thought the provision of science literature in the science area was an effective way to increase educators' science knowledge, and thereby, increase their confidence in teaching the subject. The use of science literature was also thought to support the teaching of more content knowledge as required by NAEYC Standards (2009).

Assessment of the Strategy for Developmental Appropriateness

The team confirmed that the strategy of explorer kits was developmentally appropriate for 4 to 5-year-olds. Wood, (2007) stated:

Learning goes from the hand to the head. Teachers in four-year-old classrooms need to focus on observing and redirecting behavior and asking children questions that lead them to the next level of cognitive exploration and understanding. Manipulative experiences are important in the classroom, e.g., magnets and pulleys in the science area."

Implementation of the Strategy: First Stage

The team created five explorer science kits containing materials based on Ross (2000) around the concepts of light, magnification, balance, manipulation and color. Examples of explorer kits are shown in fig 3.2

Light Explorer Kit

Materials:

- light box
- prisms
- flashlights with colanders and containers with holes
- kaleidoscopes
- light exploration box
- X-rays with matching cards
- shadow puppets

Magnification Explorer Kit

Materials:

- non-fiction illustrated books with 3D glasses
- magnetic wands
- video-scopes
- light exploration box
- X-rays with matching cards
- magnifying glasses and natural objects
- binoculars

Fig 3.2 Examples of explorer kits

Existing science materials stored in cupboards were rediscovered by the team and placed in picture and word labeled containers. Materials included colored beads, square tiles, and non-fiction illustrated books with 3D glasses. To increase the range of scientific materials, the team searched equipment catalogues and used grant funding to buy new materials to enhance the explorer kits. The team purchased a light box, light exploration box, X-rays with matching cards, prisms, magnetic wands, flashlights, kaleidoscopes, bingo-chips, scales, counting bears, video-scopes, a virtual rainmaker, colored tape, rechargeable batteries and charger, modeling dough, crystal light pulls and impression boards. The team began implementation of the strategy by creating light and magnification explorer kits, and placing them in the science area for children to use during free-play times.

Implementation of Science Explorer Kits

Fig 3.3: Children explore magnification materials

Fig 3.4: Children explore light using X-rays and the light box

After one week of implementing the strategy to provide children with light and magnification explorer kits, a 20-minute video was recorded and used to assess the impact of the strategy on children's science learning.

The Head Start Child Outcomes Framework for Science (see below) was used to analyze the video for the frequency of observed science indicators, and the team discussed questions to guide their consistent reflection.

Indicators	Frequencies
Use senses and a variety of tools and simple measuring devices to gather information, investigate materials and observe processes and relationships	40
Observe and discuss common properties, differences and comparisons among objects and materials	10

Indicators	Frequencies
Participate in investigations to test observations, discuss and draw conclusions and form generalizations	2
Collect, describe and record information through discussion, drawings, maps and charts	0
Make predictions, explanations, and generalizations based on past experiences	2
Observe, describe, and discuss the natural world, materials, living things and natural processes	2
Know about and respect their bodies and the environment	3
Know ideas and use language related to time and temperature	0
Know about changes in materials and cause-effect relationships	3

Table 3.2: The impact of explorer kits on children's science learning

The team reflected on the following questions after the video was viewed:

- Is the strategy working? How?
- Is the original teaching challenge being improved upon? How?
- Is children's learning improving? –How?
- Is your understanding of your teaching changing? How?
- Is your teaching changing? How?

Video Analysis

Sixty-two science indicators in seven categories were observed. This was almost four times the number of indicators seen on the baseline assessment video. The highest number of indicators (40) and the greatest increase involved children using their senses to explore and investigate materials and observe processes and relationships. Using the light explorer kit, children demonstrated these behaviors by looking at X-rays of animals' bones. They used binoculars and 3D glasses when they looked out of a window at people and at trees. Children observed common properties about materials as they asked each other questions about what they could see. One child said, "I can see those people even though they are way over there." Another commented on seeing the tall, green trees. Children looked at books that contained 3D pictures. They put slides in the slide viewer, and operated the lever to change the view.

On ten occasions, children explored the common properties of extending plastic pipes. They put the pipes to their mouths, blew through them, and listened to the sound they made. Children placed the plastic pipes on the floor and compared them. Two children said, "They're the same length." On two occasions, children worked together and tested materials by stretching, contracting, bending and twisting pipes into different shapes, e.g., circles, arcs, rectangles, spirals, and three sided figures. Two children remarked, "I can fold this," "I can join these together" and, "Wow, look I've made an elephant's trunk!"

Children studied how the objects in bottles of oil floated in suspension and then later settled to the bottom. They used the light box to view X-rays and gather information about animal and human skeletons. They used flashlights to shine through strainers and discover whether light would shine through the holes and land on other surfaces. In doing this, they explored changes in materials and cause and effect relationships.

Children made predictions as they passed beads through pipes and waited for them to come out the other end. They remarked, "Look at this, look inside there." One boy stretched and bent the pipe to represent a fire hose. Girls copied each other by bending the pipes into circles and then wearing them on their heads as crowns. Children watched how materials changed and made predictions about cause and effect. There were no observed outcomes for the two areas of collecting: describing and recording information; and knowing ideas and using language related to time and temperature were also needed.

Team Reflection

After watching the video, the team assessed the strategy as "highly effective" in supporting children's scientific explorations. The new science area enabled most aspects of the original teaching challenge to be improved upon. Some Head Start Learning Outcomes for Science were also met. Explorer kits placed in open baskets on shelves gave children easy access to a much wider variety of materials. The labeling of materials in words and pictures enabled children to use them independently. The new science area allowed children to discover things for themselves as the team had wanted.

Children were observed to be much more active in the new science area than they had been before. Interaction with the provided materials was thought to be critical to children's improved learning. Children liked the whooshing sound of wind that was made when they thrashed plastic pipes through the air. Educators noted how children investigated materials by viewing slides and making a rainbow with the crystal light pull held up to the light. Children were seen looking through binoculars, and discovering that they could make objects appear larger and smaller. When children wore 3D glasses they were intrigued by the red and blue lenses. When they read 3D books about bugs, they enjoyed seeing how the blurred images of the bugs stood out once they donned their 3D glasses. As children handled and showed Lite-brites, X-rays and flashlights to each other, they discussed what the purposes of these materials could be, e. g., "What is this?" "What am I supposed to do with this?" and, "How does this work?"

Children were described as curious and very interested in these materials. They discovered and recognized that they were seeing pictures of the human skeleton. The team reflected on how the children used not only their sight to explore materials, but also their combined senses of hearing and touch.

Educators appreciated the discovery element in children's learning. They supported the use of developmentally-appropriate learning methods derived through children's exploration of scientific concepts. More opportunities were created for children to use their own initiative, but at the same time, children did not have to fulfill particular expectations set by educators. The video helped educators review and remove objects and materials from the science area that impeded children's scientific play, e.g., the doll house, which was a distraction from the scientific purpose of the area. Providing children with real materials in the explorer kits enabled them to manipulate and discover properties. Educators reported that they were using both their existing and new knowledge to design challenging science activities that supported "young scientists."

The team commented that because educators were not regularly in the science area when the video was recorded, they could not tell what impact they had on each child's science learning during free-choice time. They noticed that although children asked questions about materials, no educator was on hand to answer them. While educator involvement might seem like a given, it was not. The impact of educator involvement in the science area was identified, then, as the natural focus of the next stage of the action research.

Educators determined that practices in the new science area were aligned with aspects of NAEYC Standard 5: Using Content Knowledge to Build Meaningful Curriculum.

Adult Involvement in Science Area: Second Stage of Strategy Implementation

Fig. 3.5 Educator encourages child's exploration at the light box

During the next two weeks, educators intentionally spent more time in the science area during free-play times. They supported learning goals, by implementing techniques designed to promote content teaching through open-ended discussions: asking questions, encouraging inquiry, affirming curiosity, and celebrating wonder. Using Head Start Child Outcomes Framework for Science, a third video was analyzed for observed frequencies of science indicators:

Indicators	Frequencies
Use senses and a variety of tools and simple measuring devices to gather information, investigate materials, and observe processes and relationships	38
Observe and discuss common properties, differences and comparisons among objects and materials	19
Participate in investigations to test observations, discuss and draw conclusions, and form generalizations	7
Collect, describe, and record information through discussion, drawings, maps and charts	0
Make predictions, explanations, and generalizations based on past experiences	2

Indicators	Frequencies
Observe, describe, and discuss the natural world, materials, living things and natural processes	0
Know about and respect their bodies and the environment	4
Know ideas and use language related to time and temperature	1
Know about changes in materials and cause-effect relationships	3

Table 3.3: Observed frequencies of Head Start Children's Outcomes for Science

Video Recording Analysis

With the addition of educator support, 74 further examples of science indicators in seven areas were observed in the science area. As before, children used their senses, as for example, gathering information by looking at a spider. They gathered information by looking at spider specimens through magnifying glasses.

Children used binoculars to look at each other and to look at objects outside. Children looked at X-ray images and identified them as limb bones. Children investigated materials by handling magnifying glasses, adjusting binoculars, turning spider specimens in resin over in their hands, and using construction kits to make paddles. When an educator and three children looked at books together about spiders, children's concentration was extended and their use of language was more complex.

On 19 occasions, an educator, supporting a group of children as they viewed slides, showed that they were aware of commonalities among objects. Children noticed that all spiders in the slides had eight legs. All three bottles contained different colored tornadoes and the water moved in the same way… from one end of the bottle to the other. On seven occasions, children's interest in tornado bottles was enhanced by an educator who further developed their observations into a racing game. Children explored time, by counting in seconds, which tornado lasted the longest. Children built tall structures out of the construction kit and made predictions by asking, "Look at that, it's very tall. How long will the building take to fall over?"

Children made handprints in an impression tool and showed an understanding of the characteristics of the human hand. One child shook the pins back and said, "Look, the pins don't go through your hands." The impression tool and the light box gave children many opportunities to explore how materials changed and witnessed cause and effect. The light box and X-rays gave children opportunities to learn about their skeletons. With educator support, children studied X-rays in greater detail and understood they were looking inside the body. As a group, they indicated on the X-ray where they could see a broken bone.

Team Reflection

The video clearly showed how educators' presence in the science area strengthened the impact of the strategy. Educators, as a matter of course, had a positive impact on children's science learning when they answered questions, supported discussions, read books and participated in explorations. While this outcome might seem obvious to the casual observer, it did not always register with the educators until it was put into practice.

The original teaching challenge and the strategy were improved through educators' participation in a *well-developed* science area. Children's access to varied materials was greatly improved. Science provision in the curriculum was further developed. Children's investigations were strengthened as they spent longer periods of time engaged there.

The team assessed that children's learning in the science area was naturally improving. Increased knowledge about science concepts contributed towards children's improved understanding about the materials they handled and explored. When the educator set children a challenge that required them to count backwards in a racing game, children's understanding of time was strengthened. Children's observations were more focused and more detailed when educators asked them to compare insects.

Children's concentration was extended when an educator stayed close by. The team described how one educator in the video was "very effective" because she supported children's activity, rather than taking it over. She stayed focused on children's interests and followed them with relevant comments, suggestions and sources of information to maintain their learning. A speech therapist seen in the video, identified how the richness of the science area was a good place to support a child with language delay. Previously the speech therapist had taken the child out of the classroom.

The team deduced that a well-resourced and orderly science area enabled children to make free-choices regarding the materials they wanted to explore. Each child was able to use the science area in developmentally-appropriate ways as educators had hoped. The video showed educators how science concepts explored by children during free-play times were ripe for further investigation at small-group-times. Educators identified that a better balance was needed between science provision at free-play times, and at small-group times. Both times were recognized as important in the curriculum, but building connections between science concepts during these two times of the day was new. More challenging learning opportunities could be provided to children if concepts explored during free-play and small-group-times were connected and further developed. More emphasis on science content knowledge enabled educators to plan more challenging activities for children during small-group times.

The team determined that using children's books in the science area was an effective way to support educators' lack of confidence in teaching science content. More books written specifically for children could strengthen the science content knowledge of both educators and the intended audience. Clearly, by looking at pictures and diagrams, and building related vocabulary, both children and educators expanded their knowledge, and language of abstract science concepts in particular. Educators welcomed the idea that children and educators learned and discussed science content together.

Based on what educators saw in the video, they re-examined their attitude toward the role of educators in the science area. Educators remained supportive of children's independent exploration of materials, free of predetermined learning expectations. However, educators saw how children learned even more effectively when they participated with the children in play. The team reflected that the expression, "free-play," did not mean that children's play was absent of educator involvement. This realization changed educators' perception of their role in young children's play and learning.

Over the course of the semester, attitudes improved among educators about the teaching of science. Educators not only valued children's free-play, but also recognized that educator involvement was critical to help children understand the materials they handled. Based on what children did with materials, data was entered on the video assessment grid to measure what the team still needed to do to expand science provision. To increase the level at which children could record the findings of their investigations, educators suggested that children use laminated sheets to draw pictures and diagrams, and use their early skills of emergent writing. More explorer kits were still needed to support specific Head-Start Child Learning Outcomes for Science that related to the natural world. Materials, living things and natural processes, as well as knowledge and language related to time and temperature.

Final Reflections

The team assessed that the aims of the action research had been reached through the explorer kit strategy. However, the changes were ongoing, and not all changes could be implemented during one semester. Educators saw them as gradual, and change in one area of teaching naturally had an impact on others.

Educators evolved from regarding children's free-play in the science area as the best way to build concepts (through manipulation of materials, for instance) to understanding, themselves, the value of educator participation in the process. Educators learned that they could play a critical role in helping children build science knowledge by using non-fiction books in the science area. Educators recognized that the discipline of reading on a regular basis was an outstanding way to develop their own science knowledge, and also to increase their confidence in teaching the subject.

As educators improved their science provision, videos showed initial evidence to support that NAEYC standards 1 and 5 were being met. Subsequently, video recordings contributed to meeting NAEYC Standard 3: Observing, Documenting and Assessing to Support Young Children. As a result, the teacher candidate experienced greater consistency between her learning in college courses and the practice she saw during Practicum. The teacher candidate was able to plan and implement her science lesson plan Practicum assignments in ways that were aligned with NAEYC Standards.

4. IMPROVING OPPORTUNITIES FOR PHYSICAL PLAY

Teaching Challenge

The lack of self-control in Sam, an overly active four-year-old boy.

Background

Strategy: Creating a fitness center in the classroom.

Context: The action research took place over one semester in a college campus day care center classroom with 4-5 year old children. Full day care was provided for families that worked at the college (custodians, professors and other staff), students attending the college and families that worked in the local community. During the action research, there were 16-18 children in the class, a lead educator, an assistant teacher, a teacher candidate, and a team leader.

Findings

1. The fitness center provided opportunities for Sam's physical needs to be met.
2. Sam exercised more self-control over his physical movement.
3. Sam achieved greater control when there was a purpose to his movement, e.g., moving to the beat of music.
4. Sam also showed greater self-control when he modeled physical movement for other children to copy.
5. Other social, emotional, and cultural factors outside of the fitness center affected

Sam's overly active behavior.

6. Sam commonly chose to use the center as his first activity of the morning before other children arrived in the setting.

7. Over time, Sam's ability to control his own behavior without educators' support improved.

8. With the addition of the fitness center, Sam's controlled behaviors were nearly twice as frequent as his uncontrolled behaviors.

9. Sam's relationships with other children and with educators also improved with the addition of the center.

10. Relationships between Sam's mother and the educators improved with the addition of the fitness center.

11. Educators recognized that the fitness center provided opportunities for Sam's and for other children's, physical developmental needs to be met.

12. Educators repurposed the fitness center so that Sam could use it as a self-regulation tool. This helped him use his energy so that he could focus on other activities.

13. Educators were not aware that the fitness center provided social, emotional and intellectual learning opportunities that supported children's development and learning of content.

Even as this guide defined areas for improvement, the effort to improve had a complementary, or almost parallel, impact on the teacher candidates *and* their young charges. Everyone involved benefited. This point will be illustrated again and again as we revisit the case studies that emerged in the ELC.

Educators Identify the Teaching Challenge

During the first team meeting, educators identified their teaching challenge as coping with the lack of self-control in the overly active behavior of a 4-year-old boy we will call "Sam." To investigate the teaching challenge further, the teacher candidate video-taped the boy's physical play. Educators watched the videotape during the second week's team meeting. As with other case studies the same action research protocol was followed.

Accommodating Sam's high energy level was a daily challenge. The team described Sam as a "lovable whirlwind" who was constantly on the move and unable to remain still. Educators reported the whole classroom was affected by his behavior, and wherever he went, chaos ensued. He used materials in play areas inappropriately. His most purposeful play was in the literacy area when he played with toy trains made available there.

Coping with Sam's uncontrolled physical movements was exhausting for educators. They described him as impulsive and incapable of controlling his own body. He often used his whole body inappropriately to communicate and participate in play. He twirled round and round in circles, used karate chops, kicked his feet, and threw toys around the room. He would "flop" around at circle and lunch times when he was very near other children. Sam accidentally collided with other children. He was sorry when these accidents happened, but was

Fig 4.1: The teaching challenge ~ Sam's overly active behavior

unable to control his physical behavior to suit the classroom conditions around him. Educators reported that each day, Sam slept between 1:00 PM and 3:00 PM. As he lay down, his body collapsed beneath him, and as he fell asleep, he would yell out and "flop around like a fish out of water."

Educators were concerned about maintaining a safe environment for other children. They held Sam to stop him from running in circles and presenting a physical danger to others. Safety in the classroom was a high concern for educators. Sam was a popular child and other children wanted to copy his high-energy play. However, children complained when Sam hit them accidentally. Teaching Sam self-control strategies was absolutely necessary. He was not to run in the classroom because it was dangerous to others. He had learned when the teacher said "voice," he was to lower his own voice and calm down. Sam's "hyper-kinetic behavior" compelled educators to introduce more structure into his daily routine to control his behavior.

Team Values Regarding Physical Development

Educators expected young children to be physically active, but they (correctly) considered Sam's level of physical activity to be excessive. His frenetic movement was a hazard to other children. After several years in the setting (he had been there since he was an infant) educators expected Sam to have gained some control over his movements. Control strategies were important because, if followed, they could help him manage his body movements—both now and in kindergarten, where behavioral expectations would be greater. Educators judged Sam's most purposeful play, as when he played quietly with trains in the literacy area.

The participants wondered whether Sam's busy home life had affected his behavior. He spent 45 hours each week in a childcare setting. Sam's family had moved into the area and was assimilating into a new culture. He was well mannered, respectful to others, and was already reading at a 1st grade level. Educators wondered if Sam was under pressure to fit in with new routines, unfamiliar cultural norms, and expectations for academic achievement.

Educators were also confused by the philosophy of Sam's preschool. On the one hand, this child was offered free-choice in his play, but on the other hand, Sam needed more structure to help him function appropriately in the classroom. Educators stated that Sam was an able child and a natural leader. They felt he would excel in the more structured kindergarten environment.

Aims of the Action Research

The aims of this action research were to: (1) accommodate Sam's highly active physical development needs; (2) improve indoor physical play opportunities in the setting; (3) more closely align physical development opportunities with NAEYC Standards for Early Childhood Professional Preparation Programs (2009); (4) provide teacher candidates with a Practicum field experience that was consistent with NAEYC Standards (2009) regarding physical provision and (5) improve teacher candidates' opportunities to plan and implement physical play in line with NAEYC Standards (2009).

Alignment with NAEYC Standards

The importance of teacher candidates supporting children's physical development was emphasized in NAEYC Standards (2009) Standard 1: Promoting Child Development and Learning.

Two elements of Standard 1 were relevant to supporting children's physical development. In Standard 1a: early childhood practice was based on a sound knowledge and understanding of young children's integrated areas of development, including physical, cognitive, social, emotional, language, and aesthetic development. In Standard 1c: using developmental knowledge to create healthy, respectful, supportive, and challenging learning environments to promote young children's physical and psychological health, their safety and sense of security. In Standard 5(c): Using Content Knowledge to Build Meaningful Curriculum, candidates design, implement, and evaluate curricula for each child in the following content areas: physical, language, arts, math, science, *physical* education, health, safety and social studies.

Baseline Assessment

At the start of the project, a 20-minute video was recorded to form a baseline assessment of the teaching challenge. A checklist devised by educators (see table 4.1) was used to record the nature and frequency of Sam's physical movements.

Teaching Challenge	Frequencies
Moves whole body	12
Body is uncontrolled	13
Accidentally hits children	6
High energy level unused	6
Flops around	3
Is impulsive	6
Runs in circles	2

Teaching Challenge	Frequencies
Other children unsafe	8
Plays without focus	12
Play is not sustained	8
Uses materials inappropriately	15

Table 4.1: A baseline assessment of the teaching challenge

Ninety-one examples of physical movement in 11 categories were observed. The video showed that Sam was constantly active and quickly moved between play areas. He moved in and between the discovery, house, block, library, and lunch table. His body movements were highly physical as he jumped in the air, twisted his torso, knelt down under tables, reached to get materials off shelves and placed them in cupboards. He repeatedly threw a cup with a ball in it into the air and let it fall to the floor. He upended tornado bottles filled with colored water to see the helix move from top to bottom.

Fig. 4.2: Sam on the trampoline in the fitness center

Sam's erratic movement resulted in his colliding with other children. He stood astride in a karate pose and jumped toward them. For several minutes, he pretended to empty a teapot over another child's head saying, "The yellow is the hottest." He followed this pronouncement by throwing the teapot into the air. Sam impulsively took trains from other children and threw them down on the floor. Other children were sometimes hurt when Sam lurched into them and forcibly took their toys away.

The video revealed to the team a lack of purpose in Sam's play. Rarely did his movements possess any obvious reason, and he did not develop his play into a meaningful sequence. Apart from when he played attentively with trains in the literacy center, Sam's play consisted of using materials in haphazard ways. The team reflected that although Sam was highly physical and intellectually able, he did not purposefully plan or regulate his own free play.

Selected Literature

Using key words for appropriate, the teacher candidate and college librarian searched for applicable articles. The following journal articles were selected for the team to read and to identify strategies that would help them manage Sam's physical movements in ways that promoted self-control:

(1) McCall, R. M., & Craft, D.H., (2000). Moving with a purpose: developing programs for preschoolers of all abilities. Champaign, IL. Human Kinetics.

(2) King, M., with Gartrell D. (2003). Building an encouraging classroom with boys in mind. *Young Children* 58 (4): 33-36.

(3) Leppo, M.L., Davis, D., Crim, B. (2000). The basics of exercising the mind and body. *Young Children* 78(3): 142-147.

(4) Pica, R. (2006). Physical fitness & the early childhood curriculum. *Young Children*, 61(3): 12-19.

The article by King with Gartrell (2003) was thought highly relevant to the teaching challenge. It was full of practical suggestions for physical education in the classroom. The strategy required the team to: (1) create a fitness center in the classroom that would provide Sam with physical opportunities to use his energy and learn self-control; (2) add some structure to free-play time, especially first thing in the morning to help Sam during a difficult transition time.

Educators assessed the strategy as developmentally appropriate for 4-year-olds when they read in Wood (2007) that they were,

> ...capable of almost non-stop physical gymnastics, when much learning is transmitted through the large muscles and when parents and educators need vast amounts of energy to keep up with these young dynamos (p. 47-49).

In preparation for the assembly of the fitness center, educators scouted out and procured many appropriate physical education materials. These included bean bags, a tunnel, a balance beam, a rainbow mat, a trampoline, bar, trestle table, music and movement tapes, and, an obstacle course. The team was concerned about the lack of space in the classroom. They decided to close the house area temporarily and set up a fitness center in that space.

Implementation of the Strategy: First Stage

The physical center was completed, and a 20-minute video was recorded two weeks later of Sam using the space. As educators watched the video they created a checklist (see table 4.2 below) of ten areas of desirable physical behavior that they wanted Sam to exhibit. The checklist enabled educators to record the frequency of Sam's desirable physical behaviors, and analyze the results, giving them the means to assess the impact of the strategy on Sam's physical behavior.

Desirable physical behaviors	Frequencies
Moves appropriately for situation	5
Moves purposefully	8
Moves calmly	5
Maintains reasonable space between himself and others	2
Energy used constructively	2
Movement is controlled	2
Environment is safe for others	2
Plays with focus	2
Play is sustained	2
Uses materials purposefully	3

Table 4.2: Checklist used to analyze videos and to assess the impact of the strategy

Team reflection after video is viewed:

- Is the strategy working? How?
- Is the original teaching challenge being improved upon? How?
- Is children's learning improving? How?
- Is your understanding of your teaching changing? How?
- Is your teaching changing? How?

Video Specifics

While using the fitness center, Sam demonstrated 33 examples of desirable physical behaviors in ten areas. In comparison with the baseline assessment, Sam showed more self-control in his movement. The video showed the team that he acted in ways that were more suited to the classroom situation he was in. For example, while on the trampoline, he bounced in time to music. He jumped and ran across the floor to the beat of music. He moved rhythmically to music as he "swam like a goldfish." Following music and movement instruction, he mimed cleaning his teeth. He calmly sat on a chair to put his shoes on. With another child, he lay quietly on the floor, waiting for his turn to go on the trampoline again, and then to work on the computer. He maintained a reasonable space between himself and other children, and on only one occasion, was he reminded to "keep his hands to himself."

Sam used his energy purposefully as he took his shoes off and raised his hand in anticipation of going back on the trampoline. His physical movements showed greater control and poise as he jumped high and upright and alternated his body weight from side to side. He jumped and kicked his legs out sideways like a gymnast. Sam moved backwards and forwards on the trampoline. He jumped off the back of the trampoline, away from other children, showing an awareness of other children's safety.

Team Reflections

The team was positive about the impact of the physical fitness center. The provision of high quality indoor physical play was increased and improved. Sam's highly active physical and developmental needs were met in ways that helped him regulate his behavior. Although the physical fitness center was intended primarily for Sam, it was popular among all of the children. Educators liked how materials that had been stored idly by in the cupboard were now being used. This added to the range of materials made available to *all* of the children, but because of limited space in the classroom, neither all materials, nor all play areas, could be used at the same time.

Educators reported that the original teaching challenge was improved upon. Overall, Sam used the fitness center appropriately. He repeated the activities often and, apart from him kicking his feet in the tunnel, he moved with purpose.

Sam's learning in the area of physical development was improving. He was calmer and concentrated well. Educators noticed his creative movement and said he was "a great break-dancer and was very responsive to music." When he followed instructions to "swim to the bottom of the ocean," Sam showed purpose in his movement and his play was sustained. When Sam used the trampoline, he showed social progress. He accomplished this by encouraging other children to copy his movement and using materials as he did. He said, "Do what I did and make big strides."

Educators reported how other factors, not recorded on the video, had also affected Sam's behavior. They took into account that the implementation and impact of the strategy did not happen in isolation, but was affected by other contextual factors. When Sam was reported to be sick and emotionally upset, he was inclined to scream. He also threw tantrums, forgot his coat, and lost his video. Sam jabbed another child with a train. During these episodes, the classroom was not safe for other children. Educators commented that Sam's apparent lack of proper rest made him tired, and this had resulted in his impulsive behavior. He had to be gently restrained so that other children could have a chance to toss the bean-bags. As a result, Sam's presence in the fitness center had to be closely monitored by educators.

Fig 4.3: After using the fitness center, Sam regulates his own behavior

Educators reported how they had changed the purpose of the fitness center. It was no longer only used to accommodate Sam's highly physical needs, but rather as a self-regulation tool to enable Sam to release his energy and calm down. Sam was then able to focus on other activities. One educator repeated what she had said to Sam, "I see that you have lots of energy. Do you need to throw some bean bags?" However, educators' ability to determine the impact of the fitness center on Sam's calmer behaviour was made easier than before.

Educators originally saw Sam's physical activity in the fitness center as a way for him to expend his energy so that he could then participate in other activities. They viewed physical development as a separate area. While they saw that the fitness center provided opportunities for physical activity, they did not see how it simultaneously provided valuable active integrated learning opportunities, e.g., in math, literacy, and in science content areas. Educators' comprehension of separate areas of development and discrete areas of content resulted in compartmentalized provision, in which some content areas were regarded as more important than others

Educators reported that using the fitness center as a self-regulation tool had made the classroom less stressful. They wanted to find out how often Sam used the fitness center to regulate his own behavior. Even though Sam suffered a set-back in his behavior, the team wanted to continue using the fitness center strategy because "all the kids, including Sam, loved it." While educators clearly understood the value of physical activity in the curriculum, they were not motivated to provide it. They based their decision to provide these opportunities instead based upon children's positive responses to the fitness center.

Fitness Center as a Self-Regulation Tool

Over the next week, educators counted the number of times Sam went, or was directed to go, to the fitness center. They used the tally as an indicator of his need to exercise self-control. Each day, for a six-day period, between 8:00 A.M. and 9:00 A.M., educators recorded the number of times Sam either chose, or was directed, to go to the fitness center. The following physical activities were available over the six days: hopscotch. Bean bag toss, football toss, rocking boat, and, magnetic darts. The results are shown in table 4.3.

6 Day Period	Sent by Teacher	Sam's choice
Free Play 8:00 AM – 9:00 AM	1	8
Circle Time 9:00 AM -10:00 AM	2	0
Choice Box 10:00 AM -10:30 AM	1	4

Table 4.3: The frequency of Sam's visits to the fitness center

The tally sheets showed that Sam chose to go to the fitness center eight times on his arrival in the morning during free-play. Sam chose to use the fitness center when few other children were in the classroom and more space was available. This suggested that, on arrival, Sam chose and preferred physical activities over other activities made available to him.

On four occasions, Sam chose the fitness center during choice box times. This was half as often as during free-play times. Again, Sam chose the fitness center when fewer children were around, and when more space was available for him to play.

On one occasion, during free-play time, an educator directed Sam to the fitness center to use his energy and to calm down. On two other occasions, an educator asked him if he needed to go to the fitness center, but he calmed down on his own. This suggested that Sam's reasons for using the fitness center were different from those of the educators. Sam was motivated by his preference for physical activities, whereas educators saw the fitness center as a way for Sam to use up his energy, self-regulate and then apply himself to other activities.

Educators judged "great days" as those when they did not feel the need to direct Sam to the fitness center. On those days, he was purposefully engaged in other activities. The number of times that he chose to go to the fitness center decreased over the six-day period. Sam never went to the fitness center at all during social circle times. However, the ability to determine how his visits there resulted in calmer behavior was easier.

Team Meeting in Review

When educators reviewed the tally sheet, they commented that Sam no longer needed the fitness center to control his own behavior. Sam "loved the fitness center" and like other children, eagerly participated in the ball toss, beanbag toss, the rocking boat, and the magnetic darts. Sam chose the fitness center whenever he wanted to, and was no longer upset if it was not available to him. The fitness center was clearly a positive addition to the classroom because it provided integrated physical, social, language, intellectual, and emotional opportunities for all of the children, and especially Sam, for whom it was created.

While educators were aware of the physical development opportunities offered by the fitness center, they were less aware that other developmental areas were being supported at the same time. For example, when children counted the number of times they tossed beanbags into buckets, they were naturally exploring mathematical concepts in the fitness center. This explained why educators wanted Sam to be involved in other activities in other play area that to supported his comprehensive development and learning.

Team Reflection

Educators reported that the original teaching challenge was improved upon because Sam was calmer. He did not flail around as much and did not shout out as often. He was less physical and used his words more. Sam was less frustrated and was willing to try new things, including new foods at lunchtime. Educators said Sam had better self-control.

They also reported that Sam's learning was improving. The fitness center promoted better relationships between Sam and the other children. He socialized with them more easily when he was less physical. There were fewer collisions and other children did not get hurt as often. There was less tattling about Sam because children did not need to run away from him. Educators' response towards Sam was more positive as they were more relaxed and less frustrated by his behavior. Educators enjoyed seeing him smile and were able to share jokes with him. When Sam's physical needs were met, educators' relationships with both Sam and his mother improved greatly.

Regarding educators' own professional development, their understanding of, and provision for, children's physical developmental needs improved, and were important for children's wellbeing. The video was a useful tool because it helped educators see what happened in the classroom. Events were so "in the moment" that educators could not always see what happened or what they meant. Educators said they had to take a different approach, and meet Sam's physical needs in more integrated and developmentally-appropriate ways. This included regular use and allocation of sufficient space for gross-motor materials in the classroom. Educators realized they had to change their approach to meet Sam's physical needs rather than expecting him to change his physical needs to meet their expectations about his learning and behavior.

Final Video

Fig 4.4: Sam engaged in calm purposeful play

A 20-minute video was recorded to show the impact of the fitness center on Sam's physical behavior at four different times during the day: free-play, circle time, choice box, and morning message. A total of 64 positive behaviors were observed in 10 areas:

Desirable Strategy Outcomes	Frequencies
Moves appropriately for situation	10
Moves purposefully	10
Moves calmly	10
Maintains reasonable space between himself and others	5
Energy used constructively	4
Movement is controlled	6
Environment is safe for others	4
Plays with focus	4
Play is sustained	5
Uses materials purposefully	6

Table 4.4: Video analysis to show impact of fitness center on Sam's behavior

The fact that ten frequencies were recorded in each of the first three areas of the table suggested that the fitness center was effective in meeting Sam's physical developmental needs. More examples of appropriate, purposeful, and calm physical play, showed that Sam was improving his ability to self-regulate. As a result, he demonstrated better use of space, energy, and control of movement which improved his focus, purpose, and sustained his play. There appeared to be a relationship between Sam's purposeful use of materials, and his ability to control his own behavior. When Sam was engaged in physical activity, his play was focused and sustained. At these times, his energy was used constructively and he automatically maintained a reasonable space between himself and others. During the video, 36 examples of negative behaviors in eight categories were also observed. This was approximately half the number of positive outcomes observed, and suggested that Sam was able to regulate his behavior most of the time.

Teams' Final reflective meeting

The team determined that the strategy was very successful in meeting Sam's physical development needs. Sam now took part in physical activity each day apart from when he was overly tired. This resulted in him coping better in all aspects of the daily routine.

Sam did not jump around erratically as he had before. Sam's better-controlled behavior had implications for the whole class because he was a play leader, and what he did had a ripple effect on others. Children no longer stepped back for fear of colliding with Sam.

Sam was described as more focused and stayed on one task longer. He was calmer and more in control of himself which improved his learning in all areas.

Educators commented how the fitness center strategy affected their own teaching. They understood that provision for gross-motor physical development had to be included in the daily curriculum. The two aims of the action research were largely met as the fitness center had effectively increased and improved indoor physical play provision and Sam's highly active physical development needs had been provided for. NAEYC Standards (2009) 1c: was adequately met.

Educators' awareness of the integration of physical development with other areas of development was emerging. However, an emphasis on integrated areas of development in Standard 1 caused confusion among educators who, in Standard 5(c): Using Content Knowledge were required to plan and implement meaningful curriculum in separate content areas. This separate listing of content areas made educators think that content areas should be taught separately and not integrated. As such, educators thought the fitness center provided opportunities for physical development only. They were not aware that the physical center also provided opportunities for social, intellectual, and emotional areas that they could develop into further activity, e.g., sharing, turn-taking, counting and sorting.

As physical provision was given a higher priority in the curriculum, more aspects of NAEYC standard 1c were met: Using developmental knowledge to create healthy, respectful, supportive and challenging learning environments. At the same time, the teacher candidate experienced a Practicum setting that was more consistent with NAEYC Standards and with their college methods course content regarding physical provision. Opportunities for the teacher candidates to plan and implement physical play activities were improved when a greater range of materials and sufficient space was made available. Educators recognized how movement was not just an outdoor activity, but had to be part of what children did indoors as well. Educators commented that the classrooms needed to be much larger in order for this to be done effectively.

Final Reflection

With regard to understanding Sam's learning requirements, educators reflected that movement played a crucial part in his learning and cultural needs. When his physical development needs were met, he was more able to focus and enjoy other activities too. This was apparent at choice box time when Sam played with magnets, puzzles, bottles, and books. He demonstrated self-control when he manipulated materials, e.g., doing puzzles, attaching balls to magnets, and observing the helix in the "hurricane" bottles. At circle times, he successfully participated in music and movement, and interacted with educators and with other children during singing and acting out of stories. Educators began to see that movement was best integrated throughout the whole curriculum and had to be made available to children indoors as well as outdoors. Through the video, educators observed and recognized Sam's needs and said, "We had to adapt to him and to his culture. He cannot adapt to us."

5. IMPROVING PLAY AT THE SENSORY TABLE

Teaching Challenge:

Children rarely used the sensory table.

Background

Strategy: Giving children choices of materials to develop play at the sensory table.

Findings

1. Children's sensory play was sustained at the water tray with each child staying an average of about 15 minutes.
2. When children made sailboats to use at the sensory table, their interest in playing at the sensory table increased.
3. When six children used their sailboats at the sensory table, they were interested in propelling the sailboats in the water.
4. Children used a continuous stream of language at the sensory table to explain what was happening in their sailboat stories.
5. In response to children's demands for more materials, educators used "question of the day" time to ask children about the new materials they wanted to use at the sensory table.
6. Children's concentration was sustained at the sensory table when they used materials that developed their sailboat play.
7. A social pattern was identified from one video to the next that showed how chil-

dren played together in the same groups at the sensory table.

8. Children used language and moved toys to convey meaning in their sailboat stories.

9. Sailboat play provided children with opportunities for social, physical, literacy, intellectual, creative and emotional development.

Summary

The teaching challenge: children lacked interest in, and rarely played at, the sensory table. Strategy (1) children made sailboats to use at the sensory table; (2) educators asked children to choose materials to develop their sailboat play. When children made, and used, their own sailboats they stayed longer at the sensory table.

Children suggested new materials for the sensory table. Children concentrated longer, were more social, used more movement in their play and expressed more language to create sailboat stories at the sensory table. Children's action on materials at the sensory table extensively supported their development and learning. New opportunities were created for educators to interact with children at the sensory table.

The Context

The action research took place over one semester in a rural Head-Start pre-kindergarten classroom for 4-5 year olds. Full day care was provided to children of all abilities, including those with special learning needs. During the action research, there were 16 children in the class, a lead educator, an assistant teacher, a teacher candidate, and a team leader. The High/Scope curriculum was used in the classroom.

The Teaching Challenge

Fig 5.1 Children rarely played at the sensory table

In a recorded interview, the team identified and described their teaching challenge as the need to address children's interest in playing at the sensory table during "work time." The teaching challenge presented itself in the following ways. First, the sensory table was the least-used area by children. Commonly, children played with materials available in the sensory table for a week or so, and then lost interest. There were days when no one played there.

Second, even though a varied range of materials were available, children's interest was short-lived. To sustain children's interest, educators changed materials roughly every two weeks. The following materials had been placed in the sensory table: water, dirt, sand, snow, birdseed, popcorn, beads, feathers, and table-top toys. Children especially enjoyed materials that were wet and messy.

Third, a range of tools was made available for children at the sensory table. These included spoons, pitchers, funnels, fishing poles with magnets, and containers with lids that opened in different ways. Educators were perplexed as to why these tools did not hold children's interest for any length of time.

Fourth, few children played in the sensory table, even though they had regular access to it. It was open on certain days for 45 minutes during work time. Four children had space to play at the sensory table, but it frequently was empty.

Fifth, despite educators' efforts, the sensory table was unappealing to children. They were more interested in playing in other centers in the classroom, e.g., the house, blocks, listening area, and the art area.

Team Values Regarding the Sensory Table

Educators' valued children's play at the sensory table because it provided opportunities for children to gain new experiences, and to explore new materials that supported their scientific understanding and development. Educators wanted the children to take the initiative to explore new things, and they needed new ideas that would draw children to play at the sensory table and hold their attention there.

Aims of the Action Research

The aims of the action research were for educators to, (1) develop the sensory table into an interesting play area for children; (2) increase the number of children who play at the sensory table during work-time; (3) promote and sustain children's interest at the sensory table; (4) increase the length of time each child played at the sensory table; (5) align educators' practice at the sensory table with NAEYC standards (2009); (6) improve the teacher candidate's opportunities to write and implement lesson plan assignments that reflect NAEYC standards (2009).

Alignment of Teaching Challenge with NAEYC Standards

Teaching in ways that support children's interests in their play was emphasized in NAEYC Standards (2009) Standard 1, Promoting Child Development and Learning. In Standard 1a, early childhood practice was to be based on a sound knowledge and understanding of young children. In Standard 1b, knowing and understanding the multiple influences on children's development and learning is identified as critical to successful teaching. In Standard 1c, using developmental knowledge to create healthy, respectful, supportive, and challenging learning environments is outlined. This includes spontaneous play and guided investigations; challenging learning experiences for each child; and educators encouraging children to make decisions about their own interests.

Baseline Assessment

At the start of the action research, a 20-minute video was recorded over a period of days to form a baseline assessment of the teaching challenge. The team created a video analysis checklist that included characteristics of children's current play at the sensory table. The frequency of each characteristic observed in the video was noted.

Teaching Challenge	Frequencies
Number of children at the sensory table (over 4 sessions)	11
Average time spent per child (in minutes)	10
Number of social interactions between children	5
Physical manipulation using tools and materials	41
Language use at the sensory table	18
Intellectual skills demonstrated	15
Creative skills demonstrated	6
Emotions demonstration	6

Table 5.1: Baseline analysis of the teaching challenge

The video revealed that the sensory table was not used by children in the classroom during three out of four work-time sessions. The sensory table had a small amount of water in the bottom of it, with a range of play materials lying in the water. The materials included fish, containers, jugs, and laundry container lids. The sensory table was positioned with no available storage space nearby. This meant that materials were permanently in the sensory table. The sensory table was positioned near the sink so it could be easily filled and emptied.

In footage shot following a mid-term break, the video showed 11 children played at the sensory table during one morning session. There were five girls and six boys. Individual children spent an average of ten minutes at the sensory table.

Children's social interaction was recorded on five occasions. Although groups of children played around the sensory table at the same time, much of the play was in parallel. Children showed the fish they caught using magnetic poles to other children at the puzzle table. Children left and joined the sensory area at their free will, indicating a steady flow of children through the area.

Forty-one instances of physical play were recorded. Children held fishing poles with magnets attached to them, twirled fishing lines, untangled fishing lines, poured water from containers, opened jar lids using their fingernails and teeth, unscrewed jar lids, filled containers, emptied containers, placed magnets on sea creatures, placed and lowered "caught" fish in jars.

There were 18 frequencies of children's language that commonly related to the fish they had caught. Children often spoke to themselves saying, "Oh look, I've got a pink fish!" "Hey, I've got another fish," and "I got a crab!" Another warned, "You leave my fish alone!" Children spoke about their fishing poles saying, "This cord came off." "Gosh, I can do this," and, "Oh no, I'm tangled!" Occasionally, children spoke directly to each other. While placing a magnet onto the metal ring on a fish, one child said, "Watch this, Hal. I have a fish!" While pouring from a jug into another child's jar, and holding up a crab, one child said, "Look at this!" They were all clearly excited to share their successes.

15 examples of intellectual play were recorded as children demonstrated their knowledge of counting, "I have two (fish)." "I didn't catch any." Children's knowledge of capacity was revealed when they observed a jar was full of water; used a lid to fill a jar up to "the very top;" and, observed when a jar was "half full." One child commented, "I only want a little bit of water." Another child showed his understanding of spatial concepts by saying, "My fish are on the inside (of the jar)." A child investigated motion as his fishing line twirled around his fishing pole. The child studied how it came to a standstill and asked, "Can you undo it?" As his fishing lines became enmeshed, a child attempted to untangle his. Children showed their exploration of magnetism deducing that the magnet was only attracted to the metal parts of fish. Children showed interest in buoyancy, as they noticed how fish they collected in jars floated on the surface of the water. In vain, children attempted to push fish down into the water. One child noticed that when he looked at his fish through the jar, it was magnified. He asked, "Why is it turning bigger?"

Six frequencies of creative play were recorded. While pretending to be on a fishing trip, several children stored fish they had caught in separate containers. One child fleetingly joked, "A crocodile, I've got a crocodile in here for the jar!" Another child asked, "Can I go fishing?" to which another responded, "Go fishing with animals!" Another child laughed and said, "I almost got the fish!"

Six examples of emotional development were shown when two girls shared jars. One girl remarked about another, "Chelsea was right over here. Chelsea, that was mine." Chelsea explained to the teacher saying, "I want one jar for my fish and one for the water." Chelsea was attempting to copy the play of others who after catching fish, stored them in a separate container. The teacher emphasized that children had to share materials at the water tray.

Team Reflection

On watching the video, educators were not surprised to see that the sensory table was often empty. Following the mid-semester break, when new materials were added, more children played at the sensory table. Some children stayed for up to ten minutes, whereas others stayed only three or four minutes. One child played alone for longer. While appreciating the range of learning opportunities provided at the sensory table, educators judged that because children had just returned after the break, the sensory table was again novel to them. Based on past experience, educators thought children would soon lose interest, and their play would not be sustained. Educators were not sure why children lost interest so soon. The teacher candidate added that she had never seen a single child play at the sensory table. Consequently, she was not aware that one even existed in the classroom. Educators commented that although children initially played with materials, they soon became bored.

Despite the fact that educators introduced many different materials at the sensory table, children stayed interested only for the first week or so. Existing materials included fish with and without magnets, fishing poles with and without magnets, crabs, containers with lids, laundry detergent caps and pitchers. Educators thought it was necessary to regularly change the materials to stimulate children's interest in playing there.

The team was surprised at how children used the fishing materials to solve problems in play, rather than to explore magnets in water. This was not how educators intended or expected children to play. Rather than explore scientific concepts relating to magnets in water, children were interested in creating a scenario where they stored fish in containers with twist-on lids. This suggested to educators that children were not merely interested in exploring materials, but were more interested in acting on them. Children did this by using materials, tools, and accessories to serve a purpose and to solve problems in their play. This triggered a change in educators' understanding about the nature of children's play at the sensory table.

Educators were impressed with children's perseverance in their play. Children did not give up as they attempted to attach the non-magnetic fish to a magnetic fishing pole. The video revealed that when children were interested and curious, they played for longer periods of time at the sensory table. Educators noticed how two children, in a dispute over jars with twist-on lids, managed, with adult assistance, to overcome problems with sharing materials.

Selected Literature

With the librarian's assistance, the teacher candidate selected the following articles for the team to read and to identify one appropriate strategy to overcome their teaching challenge.

(1) Church, E. B. (2006 Jan/Feb). Experiment with Water and Ice. *Early Childhood Today*. Vol 20 (4) 4.

(2) Dorrell, A. (2007). Early Childhood News. Sensory experiences can be messy fun.

(3) NAEYC. (1997) Water play, A key to children's living-learning environment. *Young Children* Vol 52 (2), 33.

(4) Szeckely, G. (2003 June). Water artists. *Children's Art Diary*.

The team reported they had already implemented some of the strategies suggested in the articles. Some experiments with water were appealing because they encouraged children's creativity. Educators commented, "Lots of good ideas to try, but a lack of materials, particularly funnels, sponges, tubes, sieves, and spray bottles prevents immediate implementation." The team was interested in trying a new strategy suggested in Szeckely (2003), Water artists. *Children's Art Diary*. Children made sailboats of their own design and then took them to the sensory table to relive actual scenes and events from their own lives. Educators commented that making boats of their own design would provide children with opportunities to recall what they had done at the water's edge over the summer. Educators would not impose upon the children any existing or predetermined ideas about the boats. In addition, educators concluded that the children could practice their cutting and language development skills through boat making. Children making sailboats and then taking them to the sensory table brought about a change in educators' practice. Until this point, educators, and not children, made decisions about materials used in the sensory table.

Team members agreed that the teacher candidate could lead the implementation of the strategy. By writing lesson plans for small-group activities, in which children made boats to take to the sensory table, the teacher candidate could fulfill part of her Practicum assignments. The teacher candidate would implement the strategy after the spring break, and would also set up the video camera, to record the impact of the strategy on children's response at the sensory table. The team would watch the video to reflect on the impact of the strategy on their teaching challenge and on children's learning.

Fig 5.2. Child makes a boat to use at
the sensory table

Developmentally Appropriate Practice

Using Wood's (2007) *Yardsticks* text, educators checked the developmental appropriateness of the boat making strategy with children aged 4 to 5 years. Wood's description of 4 to 5-year olds as active explorers and adventurers ready for everything was encouraging. The fact that children enjoy hands-on activities, manipulating materials, using tools, and exploring themes such as transportation, led the team to think that boat-making was a developmentally-appropriate strategy to increase their interest. Educators were also pleased that this strategy fitted easily into the "plan-do-review" High/Scope routine used in the classroom.

Creating an Assessment Tool

The team created an assessment grid to provide the team with a consistent focus as they viewed videos and assessed the impact of the strategy. The team identified and designed the assessment criteria that were aimed at improving the original teaching challenge seen in figure 5.1... the absence of children at the sensory table.

Implementation of the Strategy—First Stage: Children Make Sailboats

The team viewed a 20-minute video of children playing at the sensory table with their boats. The video was analyzed for examples of children's improved interest in using the table. The results of the impact of the strategy were thus:

Assessment Criteria	Frequency	Comments
Number of children playing at sensory table	8	
Children are interested	8	
Play is sustained	8	

Assessment Criteria	Frequency	Comments
Attention is held	8	
New materials explored	4	
New experiences gained	5	
Children use new language	5	

Table 5.2: Assessment grid analyzes the impact of the strategy on children's interest

Team reflection after video is viewed:

- Is the strategy working? How?
- Is the original teaching challenge being improved upon? How?
- Is children's learning improving? How?
- Is your understanding of your teaching changing? How?
- Is your teaching changing? How?
- What do we do next in our teaching? How?

Video Recording Description

Throughout the 20-minute video, eight children (six boys and two girls) played at the sensory table. Children played together in groups of five, four, three, a pair, and one child on her own. The demand to play at the sensory table was so great that it was necessary for educators to limit the number of children to four at any one time. All eight children were highly engaged in play at the sensory table. They moved their sailboats, manipulated rocks, shared and positioned other toys in the water while maintaining a continuous narrative about what was happening. Children's play was sustained with each of them staying an average of about 15 minutes. With the addition of the sailboats and other materials, children's interest was fully held with no behavior problems.

Fig 5.3 Children use their boats at the sensory table

Children explored new materials. They investigated the properties of rocks by dropping them into the water to see how much of a splash resulted; banging rocks on the sensory table base to hear the sound created; and turning rocks over in their hands to feel the surface area. Children made movements in the water that had not been seen before. A girl repeatedly moved her hands to propel the sailboats forward; steer the sailboats between rocks; create rough water during a rescue; and explore how water had been colored blue. Children gained new experiences as they used and shared other toys in the water to create play plots. In a rescue, children worked together to move people from island to island (represented by rocks) and then load them onto rescue boats. Children held silver coins in their hands to represent treasure found on the ocean bed.

Children spoke in a continuous stream to narrate their story plot. This allowed educators to understand what was happening. Hal said, "I'm crashing, May Day, May Day! I'm crashing against the rocks. Ah, you took my man. Get on my boat guys." Jack replied, "Help, mine is stuck (on the rocks) too! I can't get over." Hal replied, "No, you can't go underwater either, that's where the sharks are! He's stuck!" Jack cried, "Help, help!"

Team Reflection on the Video

The sailboat strategy was successful in increasing children's interest at the sensory table. Eight children played for almost 30 minutes during work-time. Four children made this their first choice during work-time. Boys tended to stay longer than girls. One boy spent 40 minutes playing there, and refused to come away at clean-up time. The sensory table was now used with the same frequency as other play centers.

The original teaching challenges identified were improved by the sailboat strategy. When children were given more control over their own play, their interest at the sensory table increased. Providing children with opportunities to come up with their own play plots and choose the materials they wanted to use was seen as crucial in developing children's interest.

The quality of children's learning improved at the sensory table. Children's play was more social and more animated. Language opportunities increased when children assumed their roles. Children's use of rocks at the sensory table illustrated how their learning improved in developmentally-appropriate ways. Not only did science content exist as educators had thought, but also math, literacy, creativity, and social science. Children's interest in using rocks differed from educators' ideas. Children cleverly used rocks in fantasy play to represent islands that functioned as rescue stations during shark attacks.

The team saw how the sailboat strategy sustained children's interest. The sensory table was now busy on all days when it was open. As time went on, fewer children played there, but they stayed for longer. Educators understood that a waning of children's interest was a signal for them to ask children what new materials they might want to further develop their play.

Educators reflected on how the strategy changed their understanding of their own teaching. Instead of educators making decisions about play, the children did much better when allowed to make decisions for themselves. Through decision and choice making, children became thinkers, talkers, and problem-solvers.

Educators' teaching roles changed as they became listeners and interrogators of children. Listening to children as they played was "a real eye-opener." For the first time, educators heard children's own imaginative ideas for fantasy play. When educators asked children questions, they became responsive to children's requests. New materials were chosen by children to fulfill specific purposes in play. Chosen materials created a new dynamic quality to the play. Observations of play provided the information educators needed to ask children relevant questions. When educators asked relevant questions, they, in turn, became effective supporters and sustainers of play.

Educators identified what they wanted to do next in their teaching. They were concerned they had not clearly explained the procedure they had used during circle time to help children choose new materials.

Evidence suggested that NAEYC Standards (2009) 1a, b and c were met by the sailboat strategy.

Implementing the Strategy: Second Stage

Educators thought they supported children's play more effectively when they listened, asked questions, gave choices, and helped them make decisions about materials they wanted to use. The procedure for children choosing new materials democratically consisted of educators listening to children's requests, responding by asking children to vote for requested materials, recording the number of votes cast, and announcing that the majority vote would determine which material was chosen.

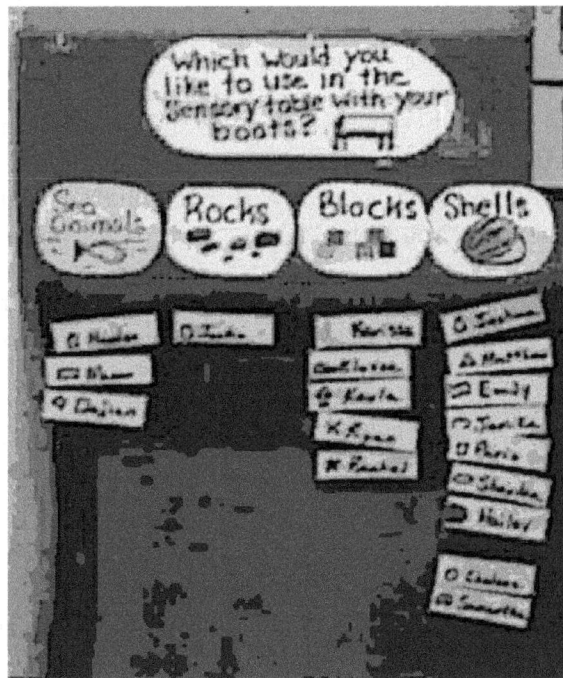

Fig 5.4 Children choose and vote on materials to add to the sensory table

Educators changed the "question of the day" to include a rotation of materials to provide children with variety. After a period of time, educators removed rocks from the sensory table, and instead, children chose to use another material. Educators explained that the material receiving the most votes would go into the sensory table. Shells received the most votes.

A 20-minute video of children playing at the sensory table was analyzed by educators. The results of the impact of the strategy of children playing at the sensory table with shells were:

Assessment Criteria	Frequency	Comments
Number of children playing at sensory table	5	
Children are interested	5	
Children's play is sustained	5	
Sensory table holds children's attention	5	
Children explore new materials	5	
Children gain new experiences	5	
Children use language skills	4	

Table 5.3: Video analysis shows the impact of using shells at the sensory table

Combinations of five children played at the sensory table (supplied with shells) which was fewer than the number that played there when the children had chosen rocks (see fig 5.3). At times, the sensory table was so full, that one child had to wait until there was an open place, which taught patience.

All five children showed interest as they played with their boats and with shells in the blue colored water. They cupped water in shells and tipped the water over each other's hands. Children made waves in the water as they steered their boats, grabbing handfuls of shells and piling them up on their boats. As they searched for shells, children said, "Look what I found," and, "You look in here."

Children's play was sustained, as on average they stayed for approximately 12 minutes each. They each brought their own boat and pretended to serve drinks to each other, like imaginary lemonade.

Children's attention was maintained as they held and observed the shape of shells. Looking at clamshells, children opened and closed the hinges. Children picked shells up out of the water, swirled them in the water and blew on them. One child felt a shell against his lip for a better sense of its texture. Children turned the shells over and, nesting them inside each other, piled them onto their boats. They gained new knowledge by comparing shells to objects with which they were familiar. One child said, while cupping water in a shell, "Looks like a medicine cup," and looking at a spiral shell, another commented, "The shell looks as if it is coming out." One child asked another to smell the shell. The child replied, "No way, I'm not smelling that!"

Team Reflection

The sailboat strategy was determined to still be working. Original teaching challenges continued to be improved upon. Regarding children's interest in playing at the sensory table, the team reflected that on days of the week when the sensory table was closed, children asked for it to be opened again. This indicated that the sensory table was now a popular play area in the classroom. On average, children stayed for about 15 minutes. Some stayed for the whole of work time, and others stayed only a few minutes. Children now played at the sensory table on a regular basis and engaged in sustained play over time.

Educators determined that children's learning was greatest when they were able to ask for and choose materials they wanted to use in the sensory table. Examples of this included asking for the water to be colored blue, and choosing rocks and shells as accessories to their boats. Regarding children's use of language, their play with boats and shells did not generate the same quantity, or richness of language, that their play with boats, rocks, and people had.

Educators believed that children's play was sustained for longer when toy versions of both people and animals were added to the sensory table activity. Children did not show the same level of creative thinking, narrative, and story plots when only inanimate objects were present. Educators believed, and rightly so, that children's attention was best engaged when the play was purposeful. The rocks enabled children to explore and be creative. The shells enabled them to use their imaginations, visualizing and using them as ballast in their sailboats, treasure, money, and medicine cups. Children gained new experiences through exploration using their senses.

Previously, children had played in parallel at the sensory table, but now educators could see them socializing and sharing. Attending to the children's use of language, the educators observed, was important. They listened to what children asked for, and noted their choices at circle time. Educators were more aware of who the askers and choosers were. They commented that responding to children's choices was "so different for us, so much more than before, when we had no clue about their ideas."

If some of this seems intuitive, it is. Their understanding blossomed from full participation in the solving of these challenges, which is the essence of the ELC.

Educators determined that: NAEYC Standard 1a-c, Promoting Child Development and Learning; Standard 3 a-d: Observing, Documenting and Assessing to Support Young Children, and elements of Standard 6b-d: Becoming a Professional were also met.

The team decided that the next stage of the action research concerned children's ability to simultaneously choose multiple new materials to add to the sensory table.

Implementing the Strategy: Third Stage

Fig 5.5 Children use a collection of new materials

A 20-minute video showed three sequences; (1) at circle time when children chose materials from four choices and voted to add sea creatures; (2) a group of boys playing at the sensory table and; (3) a group of boys and girls playing at the sensory table. The video clips were analyzed using the assessment grid criteria. The results of asking children to choose new materials were as follows:

Assessment Criteria	Frequency	Comments
Number of children play at sensory table	8	Two groups of four
Children are interested	8	All fully involved
Children's play is sustained	6	With more materials
Sensory table holds children's attention	6	
Children explore new materials	8	
Children gain new experiences	8	
Children use language skills	8	

Table 5.4: Video analysis shows impact of children choosing new materials

During the two video clips taken at the sensory table, eight children were seen playing there. The number of children that played with their sailboats was highest when toy people and animals were made available. All eight children showed interest in playing simultaneously with sailboats and sea animals like crabs, fish, sea horses, shrimp, and sharks. Boys collected their sailboats before coming to the sensory table. One boy made two boats, a second boy exclaimed, "I'll get my new one," and a third boy made engine noises as he steered his sailboat through the water. The boys showed interest as they "fished" for sea animals. One said, "I'm going fishing. I caught something." They piled sea creatures on each other's boats which naturally elicited some complaints. Children's active play was enhanced when the plot was dynamic.

Children's play was also sustained. Some children stayed 15 minutes, while others stayed only ten, but then returned later. Others stayed just three minutes. The same children were seen repeatedly on the video. This suggested that these were regular players at the sensory table who continued their play with the same friends from one session to the next. This suggested that those same children developed their play plots over time. When children heard music that signaled the end of work-time and time to clean up, one said, "Oh, we were doing fine. We had fun". This showed that children wanted to continue to play there for longer.

Children's interest and attention were held throughout their time at the sensory table. Interest and attention appeared to be maintained through social interaction between children as they noticed that some fish "were the same." Others made up and narrated stories of hammerhead shark attacks that "cut" into their boats. One child's interest and attention was held as she searched for treasure in the water and sorted it into different piles on her boat. Children did not explore the toy sea creatures in the same way that they had with the rocks and shells. Instead they used sea creatures, specifically sharks, to make up stories about shark attacks.

Children's new play plots were significant because of what they did with the toy sea-creatures. They knocked their own heads with the hammerhead sharks, symbolizing how an attack would take place. Children placed the hammerheads under their boats, symbolizing an attack, and one child even placed a person on the top of the sail mast of the boat, to represent an escape route! A boy played with a seahorse and said "giddy up" as he attacked another child's boat!

The play shark attack gave the educators a chance to observe the children's language skills and their ability to convey meaning. One child said, "The shark will catch me." A second replied, "What do I do? The shark is in the boat!" A third added, "The shark's going to cut my boat. Help me, the shark will catch me. Ah, ah, the shark is biting my fingers!" A girl exclaimed while searching for treasure, "Oh no, I've dropped my treasure. What can I do?"

Team Reflection

The team reflected how the strategy had increased children's use of the sensory table over the course of the action research. At the start, few or no children played there, but their numbers had increased to an average of eight children each session. There had been days when the sensory table had been completely full. The number of children tended to peak by the third day and then trail off. To maintain numbers at the sensory table, educators knew to ask children what materials they wanted to add next.

Educators remarked that the original teaching challenge had been improved upon. The *key* to maintaining children's interest lay in offering them choices for what they wanted to play with at the sensory table. Educators said children were only interested in the sensory table for short periods of time. However, the boat-making activity, for instance, had extended the interest of all children who played at the sensory table.

"Question of the day," where children were asked to choose and vote on materials had been successful. It appeared that providing children with choice and decision-making opportunities was instrumental to maintaining their interest. Children's play was sustained at the sensory table from about ten minutes per child to about 13 minutes per child. Both boys and girls now chose to play there regularly and stayed for longer periods of time.

New materials also increased children's attention at the sensory table. Educators said the children learned more and used all five senses, making up imaginative stories, with increased social involvement and more use of language. Children's exploration of these materials was a major feature of the project. The educators wondered why they had added different materials to other centers in the classroom, but not to the sensory table. However, children's own input was what had made the difference, along with educators' belief about the importance of hands-on learning, investigation, and active learning. The critical element included educators asking children questions about the materials they wanted.

Educators remarked that they had to support children's ideas by changing aspects of their own teaching. Children gained new experiences by coming up with their own ideas and then using them at the sensory table. Educators already knew to observe children and follow their interests. They now realized they also needed to get children's input to determine what aspects of practice would benefit from change.

Educators' improved practice, brought about by their deeper knowledge and understanding of young children's thinking in fantasy play, resulted in a sound base for responsive practice. The influences that affected children's development and learning were better understood, resulting in children choosing and acting on materials to reveal the plot and meaning in their play. Respectful learning environments resulted in beneficial support, challenge, and opportunities, with each of these enabling children to make decisions in their play. The video camera showed educators the real activity of children at the sensory table and helped educators promote positive learning outcomes. Educators became professionals when they engaged in collaborative action research, and when they were able to reflect and express their new understanding of their teaching.

The teacher candidate benefitted from the improved consistency that existed between the content learned in college classes, and the practice experienced in the Practicum classroom. Participation in the action research gave her consistent knowledge, confidence, and the support to carry out lesson plan assignments designed to improve children's learning opportunities. Evidence suggested that NAEYC Standards (2009) 1, 3, and 6 were met by the sailboat strategy.

Final Reflection

The aims of the action research were fulfilled. The boat-making strategy was successful in making the sensory table a more interesting and frequently used play area. The number of children at the table was increased by the implementation of the boat making-strategy. Children's interest was sustained as they developed their own fantasy play plots, and groups and individuals played at the sensory table for longer periods of time.

Alignment with NAEYC standards was improved when educators worked with a deeper understanding of the characteristics and needs of 3 to 4-year-old children. Educators worked more closely with children by providing them with opportunities to choose materials for the sensory table. However, children's free choices were not guaranteed until educators gave them daily access to the sensory table, and multiple materials were stored and made accessible in close proximity to it. Healthy, respectful, supportive, and challenging learning opportunities were provided to support spontaneous play. However, more opportunities to use content knowledge were needed to further develop children's learning. Closer alignment with NAEYC standards, in both college courses and in Practicum, created consistent opportunities for the teacher candidate to design and implement high quality assignments.

Team values changed incrementally over the action research. Educators retained their values about the importance of children learning through exploration of materials. However, new values were formed when educators learned that children had highly creative ideas of their own for their play. Children needed to have access to a broad range of resources that they could utilize to give their play meaning. These ideas enabled children to develop new skills in language, imagination, plots, purpose, investigations, decisions, and problem-solving. The team realized that their role was to expose children's ideas in play, and support them in their endeavor to build concepts during sensory table play at circle and work-times.

6. BOYS' CAPACITY TO EXPRESS EMOTIONS

Teaching Challenge

Boys are unable to express their emotions appropriately.

Background

Strategy: Implementing a guidance plan to support boys' communication skills.

Summary

The team devised a guidance plan comprising "The Five Finger Method of Conflict Resolution" and a "Feelings Chart." The purpose of the guidance plan was to support educators' use of certain methods with a group of 3-year-old boys with delayed speech. Educators aimed to encourage appropriate behavior among the boys through positive communications during play. By following the guidance plan, educators became more responsive to the boys' needs while being less controlling. A problem-solving approach to behavior management enabled educators to communicate more effectively, and resulted in a less stressful classroom. When boys showed more interest and engagement in their play, their behavior improved.

Pointing to relevant images on the feelings chart during circle time gave the boys a way to express their emotions. Educators changed their behavior management role from disciplinarian to facilitator of play. Most educators realized that developmental knowledge of 3-year-olds's feelings at a given moment was critical to their effective behavior management. Other educators resisted new guidance strategies, and required more time to gain professional knowledge in order to implement developmentally-appropriate practices.

The Context

This action research took place over one complete semester in a classroom for 3-year olds enrolled at a daycare center in a small city. Full daycare was provided to children of all abilities, including those with exceptional learning needs. In a classroom with a lead educator and an assistant educator, ten of the 16 children were boys.

The New York State Common Core Standards in use at the time were used in the setting to guide the curriculum and learning outcomes.

Teaching Challenge

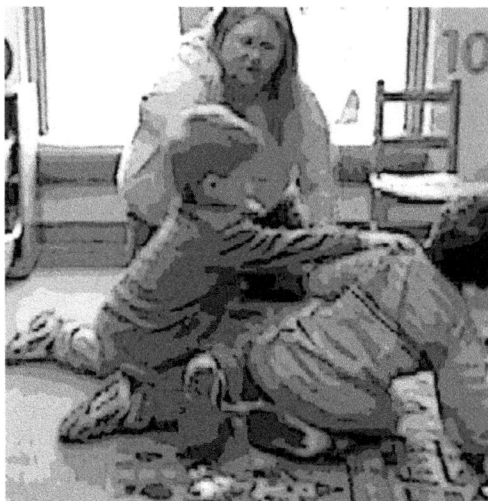

Fig 6.1: Managing the difficult behavior of 3-year-old boys

During the first team meeting, educators identified their teaching challenge as managing the difficult behavior of a group of 10 three-year-old boys. To gather data to investigate the teaching challenge further, the candidate video recorded the boys during free-play. During the second week's team meeting, educators watched the videotape. The following paragraphs are a record of the comments educators made while watching the footage. The narrative includes a description of the teaching challenge and reveals educators' own beliefs about the boys' behavior problems.

For various reasons, the boys' delayed speech contributed toward difficult behavior. Many boys spoke at a two-year-old developmental level. One boy was an English language learner. As a result, communication problems arose between the boys and educators. Boys, unable to fully understand what was said to them, could not express themselves clearly either. Delayed speech development meant the boys tended to express their feelings and needs physically by hitting and kicking others.

The boys were highly physical which made it hard for educators to maintain their interest in activities. Rather than use classroom play centers in the ways that educators intended, the boys ran between centers, used materials for unorthodox purposes, and played highly physical games like "Spiderman." In a small classroom, the boys created a commotion, as they touched each other, and wrestled on top of each other. As they ran on a gravel path, when they were allowed to go outside, accidents occurred.

Boys' under-developed social skills also contributed to the teaching challenge. They often played in parallel, i.e., in proximity to one another, but not interactively in social play. Disputes over toys were common because boys did not share toys. This was exacerbated further because there were not enough toys or materials available. The boys were limited in their ability to make play choices.

Team Values

Educators did not want to stereotype or label the boys because of their delayed language, poor concentration, and under developed social skills. However, educators judged that many of the boys *were* developmentally delayed, and immature for their age. By comparison, 3-year-old *girls* were perceived to be more mature and were positive role models to the boys. The lack of girls in the class seemed to impact boys' behavior by the absence of their positive influence. Educators wondered how to improve their behavior management skills. They said they needed help in creating smoother transitions and routines in the classroom that would help improve boys' behavior. The adult to child ratio of 1:7 increased the likelihood that educators would spend a lot of time "putting out fires" in the classroom. Rather than directing and correcting boys' difficult behavior, educators wondered how they could support appropriate behavior. Educators thought that the boys' difficult behavior needed to be "ironed out now," to help them make a successful transition to the next class when they would be 4-year-olds.

The educators thought the boys needed more time to play to support their development. Knowing how to create appropriate play provision and behavioral expectations for boys who were developmentally delayed was difficult. Educators wondered about using signing in the classroom to improve their communication with the boys. Questions arose about whether existing materials were appropriate and interesting to the boys. During outdoor play, educators noticed how boys enjoyed watching jet-trails in the sky. However, educators needed help in knowing how to use this experience to create learning activities that engaged boys' interests.

Aims of the Action Research

The aims of this action research were to: (1) improve educators' interactions with 3-year-old boys; (2) create a guidance plan that would help educators develop beneficial interactions with them; (3) provide the teacher candidate with consistent opportunities that connect the theory of developmentally-appropriate interactions with boys, taught to them in college classes, with educators' practice in Practicum; and (4) improve the teacher candidate's opportunities to plan and implement lesson plans in ways that demonstrated NAEYC Standards (2009).

Alignment with NAEYC Standards

In NAEYC Standards for Early Childhood Professional Preparation Programs (2009) interactions with children are required to be grounded in a child development knowledge base, one that is deeply linked to a sympathetic understanding of each young child (Elkin, 1994). In Standard 1: Promoting Child Development and Learning, teacher candidates are required to demonstrate an understanding of each child's characteristics and needs and provide for their physical, cognitive, social, emotional, language, aesthetic, play, learning processes, and motivation. Teacher candidates are required to demonstrate an understanding of the multiple influences on the development and learning of each child, including their cultural and linguistic relationships with adults and peers, economics, health, disabilities, individual development, learning styles, play, technology, and family and community characteristics. Teacher candidates are required to demonstrate, using developmental knowledge, healthy, respectful, supportive, and challenging learning environments for each child. They are expected to do this by recognizing them as feeling, thinking individuals whose abilities, family contexts, home cultures, and languages are to be affirmed. Each child must have opportunities to learn through play, spontaneous activity, and guided investigations.

The Baseline Assessment

Using the educators' description of the teaching challenge, the team created a checklist of 11 difficult behaviors to form a baseline assessment of their teaching challenge. A 20-minute video was recorded of the ten boys during story time, outdoor play, and free indoor play. While watching the video, educators used the checklist to count the frequency with which each difficult behavior occurred. The checklist was used as a consistent assessment tool throughout the action research.

Teaching Challenge	Frequencies
Child is not interested in activity	8
Child has under developed speech	3
Child does not listen	2
Child shows physical frustration	3
Child plays in parallel	5
Child shows anti-social behavior	0
Child does not share	0
Child makes erratic transitions	0
Child has insufficient materials	1
Educators direct boys	8
Educators have developmentally inappropriate expectations	3

Table 6.1: Baseline assessment of the teaching challenge

Thirty-three examples of boys' behavior were recorded on the video and analyzed. All eight examples of boys not being interested were observed during story time, when boys sat on a rug, listened to a CD about farm animals, sang along with the CD, made animal noises, and moved like the appropriate farm animal. It was difficult to maintain boys' interest in the activity when they were expected to sit and listen to the CD. The frequency of boys not being interested in activity correlated to educators directing their play.

Some boys did not speak in complete sentences. On three occasions, boys gave partial instructions to each other about what to do with trucks, and where to put them during clean-up time. Three examples of physical frustration were evident as boys climbed onto an off-limits climbing frame and, when in play, they threw stones. Five examples of boys' parallel play were seen outdoors as they drove trucks in the gravel and then assembled a railway track. No examples were observed of boys' anti-social behavior, not sharing materials, or erratic transitions. As boys played with bricks, there was one example of insufficient bricks being made available. On eight occasions, educators directed boys' behavior with the aim of maintaining their interest in their activities. During these times, educators directed where boys should or should not be, e.g., "You can't go under the structure. It is not safe." Educators responded to boys by asking questions, e.g., "Who is throwing stones? What shape is the track? What color is that?" There were three examples of when educators restricted where boys could move to and also restricted the range of play materials they could use.

Team Reflection of the Baseline Assessment

The team reflected that although the video showed chaotic incidents, like a child crashing into another with a truck; a second child taking a toy from another; a third child hitting another, the video did not show the "overwhelming" problems educators faced maintaining to make boys' interest in activities. Although no evidence was recorded that showed *all* categories of difficult behaviors, the video revealed that educators spent considerable time lecturing, directing, and correcting boys' behavior in a bid to improve it and to maintain their interests.

The team believed the boys needed a structured routine to improve their interest in activities. The team also noticed the boys' difficult behavior was not exclusively about their lack of interest in activities, but was, more often, an expression of negative emotions. Based on this new insight, educators re-conceptualized the teaching challenge from improving boys' difficult behavior to increasing opportunities for boys to appropriately express their negative emotions. Educators already knew that, because of their under-developed language skills, boys used their bodies to express negative feelings. Educators realized the boys' difficulty in maintaining interest in activities was often connected to them not having the words or social skills to express emotions appropriately. Educators expressed frustration that a policy did not exist in the setting to address this concern. The lack of a policy resulted in educators "winging it," which they said explained their uncoordinated, reactive, and inappropriate responses to the boys' learning and development needs.

Selected Literature

Assisted by the librarian, the teacher candidate selected three articles for the team to read. The articles were related to helping boys to express emotion appropriately:

(1) Fox, L., and Harper Lentini, R. November (2006). Teaching boys a vocabulary for emotions. *Beyond the Journal – Young Children. naeyc.org*

(2). Fox, L., and Harper Lentini, R. November (2006). "You got it!" teaching social and emotional skills. *Beyond the Journal – Young Children. naeyc.org*

(3) King, M. & Gartrell D., (July 2003) Building an encouraging classroom with boys in mind. *Young Children Vol 58 No.4.*

(4) Gartrell, D. (2002) Replacing Time-out. Part Two – Using guidance to maintain an encouraging classroom. *Young Children* Vol 57 No.2.

The team chose three strategies, two articles, *Teaching Boys a Vocabulary for Emotions,* and *Replacing Time Out,* because both articles closely matched their teaching challenge. The team used the articles to write their own policy for supporting boys' emotions. The chosen strategies were: (i) The Five Finger Method of Conflict Resolution (ii) the Guidance Talk and; (iii) a feelings chart.

The Five Finger Method of Conflict Resolution

The Five Finger Method of Conflict Resolution (See figure 6.2) consisted of five steps for educators to follow when approaching and supporting a child in a situation of conflict. The steps were:

1. Cool down – the educator calms all individuals, including him or herself, and sets the scene for the remediation process.
2. Identify the problem – the boys, with help from the educator, put the problem into words and agree on what it is.
3. Brainstorm solutions – the boys, with help from the educator, are given a chance to solve their own problems. Educators get down to their level, act as a role model for appropriate behavior, and use an encouraging voice.
4. Go for it – boys and educators decide on one solution and try it. The educator shows respect for child autonomy and gives compliments in support of ideas.
5. Follow up – the educator encourages, monitors, and guides the boys as they try out the solution. A guidance talk with the boys may be part of this step.

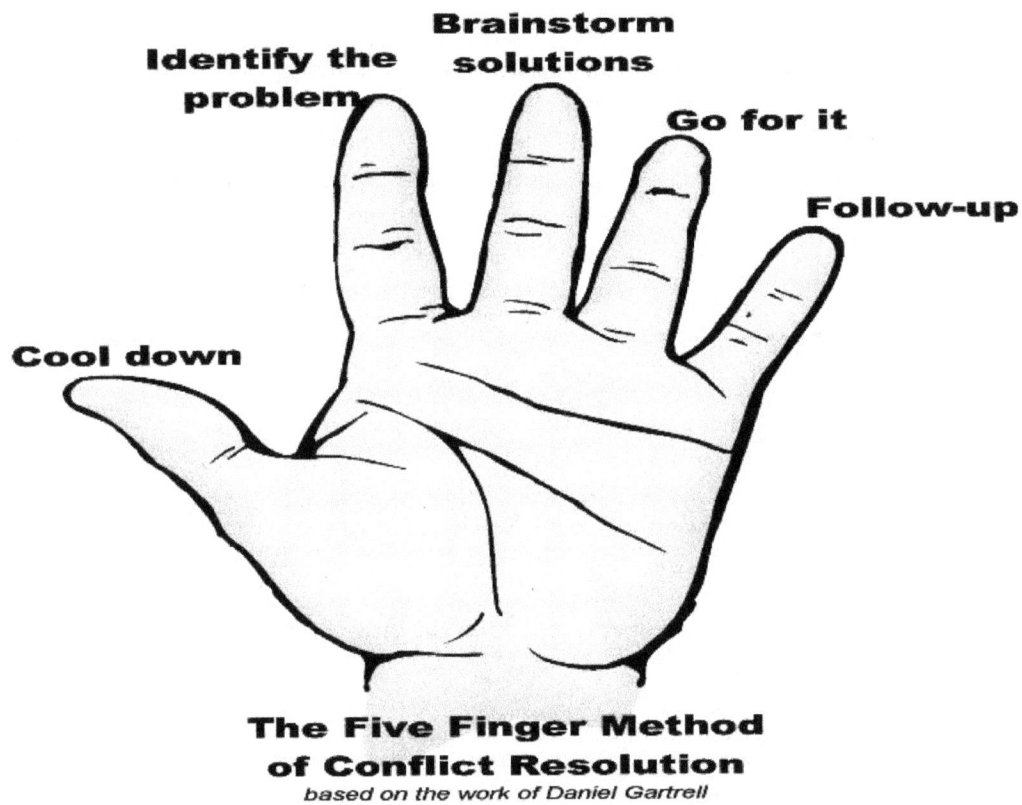

Fig 6.2: The 5 Finger Method of Conflict Resolution

Guidance Talk

Following the use of the Five Finger Method of Conflict Resolution, and adapted from Gartrell (2002), educators carry out the guidance talk privately with a child to avoid embarrassment. This consists of talking *with* a child and not *at* a child. The purpose is to teach the child that they can respond differently in conflict situations, and to provide the child with alternatives. During the guidance talk the educator will:

1. Discuss what happened during the conflict and convey to the child why the behavior was mistaken. For example, it is appropriate to feel frustrated when the glue bottle top comes off, but it is not appropriate to throw the glue bottle and hit someone.
2. Help the child understand how others may have felt. A goal is to build empathy in the child.
3. Brainstorm with the child alternative acceptable behaviors to use the next time, e.g., "Next time you can say, don't do that – it makes me angry."
4. Ask how the child can help the other child feel better. This is different from forcing an apology. Neither boys nor educators benefit when they are forced to apologize before conflicts are resolved. When boys participate in reconciliation, they are usually more able to make amends. Boys often come up with their own ideas for getting back together.

The Feelings Chart

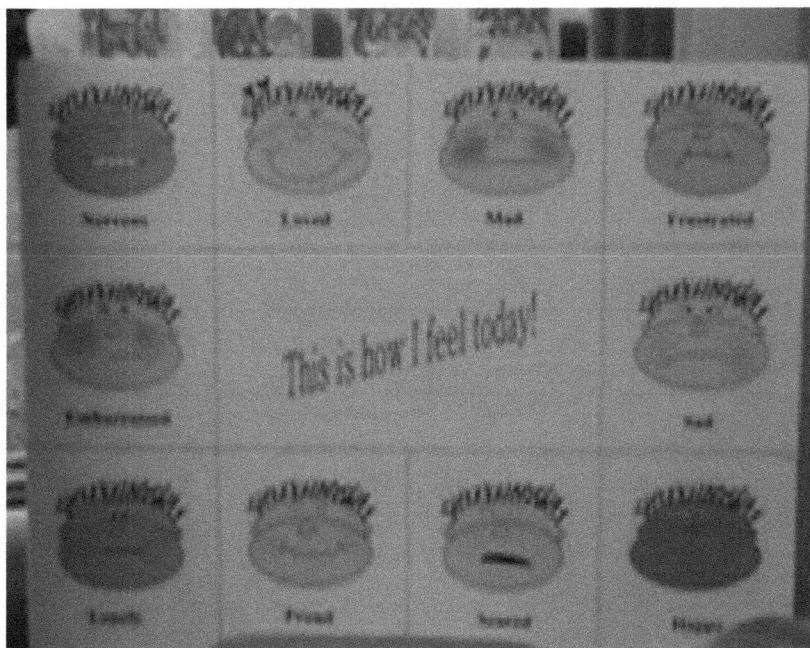

Fig 6.3: The Feelings Chart gives ten options for expression

The team agreed that a "feelings chart" could be introduced to the boys at circle time. The chart was designed to help the boys explore a range of emotions, identify related facial expressions, learn appropriate vocabulary, and connect those words to their own feelings. Boys were thought to know the vocabulary for the extreme emotions of happy and sad, but they did not yet know the words for a range of other emotions in between.

Writing the Guidance Plan

As the team started to write their guidance plan, some educators had difficulty in understanding the concept of "guidance" to help the boys express emotions appropriately (Gartrell, 2007, p.24). Their earlier practices were commonly based on reprimand and prevented some educators from understanding how to use guidance to help the boys. Changing the understanding of some educators about how to support boys' emotions did not happen easily. The implementation of the guidance plan strategy was delayed. Some educators said it was "second nature" for them to use reprimand and directional strategies.

These educators did not initially understand that behavior management methods had to be based on child development principles so 3-year-olds would understand them. (Copple & Bredekamp, 2009) This was particularly important when some of the boys appeared to be developmentally delayed. One boy's comment illustrated this child development principle through his pre-operational understanding. He asked, "If the thinking chair is not here today, does it mean that no-one will be bad?" The guidance plan had to be simple to enable educators to implement it consistently, and for them to be confident that it would improve the teaching challenge.

Implementation of the Strategy: Stage 1 – Writing the Guidance Plan

The team based their guidance plan on Gartrell's (2007) philosophy. The philosophy stated that preschool boys don't misbehave; instead they have "mistaken behavior." In other words, boys are learning social skills to participate in group activities and to interact with one another. Their learning isn't always perfect, and they need guidance in learning social skills. Gartrell contended that boys need to learn appropriate behavior with the same gentle instruction that we use to teach new words. With this in mind, the team wrote the following guidance plan:

The Guidance Plan

When guiding boys' behavior, educators plan to take the following steps:

- Assess the situation. (Is the situation dangerous?)
- Provide boys with chances to solve problems on their own if possible.
- Help promote problem solving, if boys aren't able to find their own solution.
- If boys are visibly upset and unable to solve a problem peacefully, separate them and allow them to calm down. Stay with the child at this time.
- When boys have calmed down, discuss the problem and get the boys to give ideas about how the incident could have gone better.
- All staff must model appropriate behavior to the boys. It is important for the educator to get down to the child's level whenever necessary to interact appropriately.
- Use the chart to support boys' use of feeling words and to increase boys' awareness of their impact on others.

Table 6.2: The Guidance Plan

A video was recorded that showed educators using steps 1 – 6 of the guidance plan; step 7 of the Feelings Chart; and the impact these strategies had. The team developed a second checklist in which the negative teaching challenges in the first checklist were reversed into positive guidance plan outcomes. The team used this list to analyze the tape by counting the frequency of boys' appropriate expressions of emotion.

Guidance plan outcomes	Frequencies
Interested in activity	6
Communicates with others	6

Fig 6.4: Educator uses the Guidance Plan to help child problem-solve

Guidance plan outcomes	Frequencies
Listens to others	5
Expresses feelings appropriately	7
Socializes appropriately	4
Social behavior	5
Shares with others	4
Smoother transitions	2
Accesses materials appropriately	3
Responds to guidance	4
Problem solves	6

Table 6.3: Checklist used to analyze impact of the guidance plan strategy

Team reflection after video is viewed:

- Is the strategy working? How?
- Is the original teaching challenge being improved upon? How?
- Is children's learning improving? How?
- Is your understanding of your teaching changing? How?
- Is your teaching changing? How?

Video Recording Analysis

While using the guidance plan strategies with four boys playing with a circular train track and toys, 52 frequencies of guidance plan outcomes in 11 categories were observed. The educator facilitated the boys' interest, as she sat close to them and supported their play with the train track. The educator helped boys communicate over a problem concerning sharing the train track and not pushing Jake's train off. The educator asked the boys questions about what happened when Jake's train was pushed off. She gave the boys time to explain the problem from their own perspectives. Jake said, "On my train track—he pushed on my track." When the educator created a climate in which boys were given opportunities to talk, other boys were able to listen, although they did not always respond. The educator commented that Charlie was not ready to talk yet.

The educator provided many opportunities and extended time for the boys to express their feelings about the train track problem. She asked, "How did that make you feel? We don't throw toys because someone could get hurt." The boys used words that were on the feelings chart, e.g., sad, and phrases that included, "I don't like that." For the most part the boys socialized appropriately and were not physically abusive to each other.

Boys' positive feelings and behavior were further supported when they were able to choose materials for themselves and perform actions. When boys were able to access and perform actions on toys, smoother transitions in play resulted. Some boys hoarded trains in front of them, but as long as there were sufficient toys for each boy, a problem did not develop.

The educator used guidance to help boys think about problems concerning sharing toys. She asked each boy in turn how he felt, and provided him with possible strategies he could use to help the matter, e.g., "You could say, 'please don't take my toy now, but when I am done, you can play with it.'" Problem-solving was effective when the educator encouraged the boys to be empathetic and consider how their action affected others.

Team's Reflective Meeting

Team discussion suggested the guidance plan was working. Kinder and more positive interactions occurred between educators and boys in the classroom. Boys were more able to express themselves by asking or indicating before they did things. Educators praised them as a form of positive reinforcement.

The original teaching challenge was being improved upon through successful implementation of a guidance plan that was found to be dependent upon educators' communication skills with boys. Educators' use of language had to be clear and specific in order to draw out boys' ideas about behavior problems and offer suitable solutions that could be used.

When educators consistently used the guidance plan, children's learning improved. When educators communicated with boys in ways that built empathy and modeled respect, children were more responsive. Circle time was recognized as effective to consistently model the use of the guidance plan to all the boys. Open-ended questions were helpful, e.g., "What's the problem? What can we do to sort it out?" Educators recognized they had to acknowledge boys' feelings in ways that helped them to problem-solve. Educators realized that they had to be aware of the possible causes of behavior problems, such as home lives and cultures. They needed to have an understanding of typical child development for 2- and 3-year-olds and be aware of the implication of boys' immaturity, and the need to use developmentally-appropriate responses.

Some educators, however, found it difficult to implement the Five Finger Method of Conflict Resolution. They said they needed more time and practice to feel comfortable using it. Changing practice was a process that took more time than was recognized. Bringing the guidance plan down to the boy's level of understanding was a challenge. This finding indicated that educators' own communication skills, and the use of appropriate vocabulary, were critical to successful implementation. The team used role-play during team meetings to give them practice and confidence in using it.

Understanding educators' concerns about using the guidance plan was important in supporting their professional development. Some educators asked questions about when and how they should intervene during problematic behavior. Others said they found talking to, and interacting with, highly physical boys difficult. Educators did not believe that guidance worked without reprimanding boys to point out their mistakes. Some educators preferred to use distraction as a way to prevent behavioral problems. They thought that boys screamed for attention, and *expected* to be punished when they behaved badly.

Educators' changing approach regarding behavior management was a process that would take time to become embedded in their professional practice. (Copple & Bredekamp, 2009) One educator remarked that the change was radical saying, "I'm lost for words—this is a whole different take for us." Up to this time, some educators appear to have used personal rather than professional knowledge to manage children's behavior. Parents noticed that guidance, rather than "time out," was being used in the setting. Some parents talked to educators about the changes and said they no longer used a "time-out" chair at home." The impact of new guidance behavior management practices in the classroom was spreading into children's homes.

The video was used to record the effectiveness of the feelings chart, the frequency of boys using feeling words, and boys' awareness of their impact on other boys in the classroom.

Feeling Chart Outcomes	Frequencies
Interested in activity	10
Communicates with others	6
Listens to others	4
Expresses feelings	4
Socializes appropriately	5
Social behavior	4
Shares with others	2
Smoother transitions	1
Accesses materials appropriately	8
Responds to guidance	6
Problem solves	1

Table: 6.4: Video analysis of the impact of the feelings chart on children's behavior

Video Recording Description

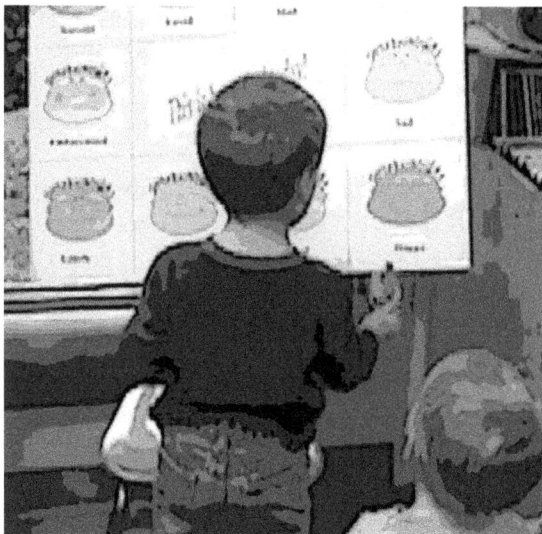

Fig 6.5: Child uses feelings chart to express emotion

During circle time, when an educator used the feeling chart as a game, boys demonstrated 51 positive behaviors in 11 categories. The boys were very interested in the activity that invited them to say how they felt, and select a face on the chart that matched their feelings. Boys' interest in the activity was maintained, especially when they manipulated pegs, and placed them on the appropriate face of the feelings chart. Boys communicated appropriately as they listened to the educator, and to each other, talk about their feelings. Each boy had a peg of his own and this resulted in the activity being successfully implemented. The boys socialized appropriately and crowded around the chart to see where others had put their pegs. To avoid waiting, some boys who had placed their pegs earlier, went to the bookshelf to look at books and waited until all the boys had placed their pegs on the feelings chart. The educator summarized how many boys had said they were mad, proud, scared and happy. She also reminded the boys that, if their feelings changed, they could come and change where they placed their pegs.

There was only one example of when boys, with the educator's help, used the feelings chart to solve problems. This was when one boy's feet got stepped on while placing pegs on the chart. This incident suggested that, at this beginning stage, boys used the feelings chart to express their own feelings, rather than to explore the feelings of others.

Team's Reflective Meeting

Educators' responses to the implementation of the feelings chart were positive. They reported that "it's working because the pictures help the boys use more words in their play."

Reading about the feelings chart in the journal helped educators understand how it supported boys' thinking and explained why it worked. As a result, many aspects of the original teaching challenge were improved. Educators reported how the classroom felt calmer and less hectic. Educators were less controlling and fewer rules were imposed to keep order. Boys were given more freedom to make choices in their play and to act on materials than before. However, one educator still believed that it was important to have rules to maintain a safe classroom environment.

The team reported that working with the feelings chart made them more aware of boys' learning needs. One journal article had indicated the need for boys to have fine and gross-motor movement throughout the curriculum. This led to team discussion about the daily schedule and whether blocks of time were used to create the best physical play opportunities. The problem of having to share the gross-motor room meant that half-hour blocks of time were not as effective as previously thought. Educators realized it was important to organize time, so boys had enough time to make choices about materials and decide how they would use them. Some educators voiced concern that too many boys in centers at one time made it necessary to rotate the boys between centers with timers and rules.

Reflecting on the use of the guidance plan, educators said they now found it better not to use "time out" and, instead, preferred to help boys solve their own problems. Using problem-solving strategies helped boys make more decisions themselves, and say, "I'm ready to go back in and play. I'm ready to talk now." Educators commented that using the guidance plan had made it necessary for them to "program their own brains, too."

Although some educators continued to grapple with changed practice, and needed more time to make adjustments, most educators' values about behavior management changed significantly. They changed from believing that *gender* and maturity determined child behavior, to understanding how multiple factors affected each child's individual development. Reading journal articles equipped educators with a deeper knowledge of child development in 3-year-olds. The guidance plan supported educators' teaching actions in ways aligned with the development of 3-year-olds. Most educators realized that their professional knowledge, and not their personal knowledge, was key to them effectively supporting children's behavioral needs. These involved educators responding to the boys' current emotional, language, and social development (Copple & Bredekamp, 2009). The impact of educators' improved practice was copied by some parents at home. More consistent behavioral norms were created for children when the same improved practices were used both in the preschool and at home.

The director was regularly involved throughout the action research semester. She played a critical role in supporting educators to consistently implement the guidance plan. She reported how other educators in other classrooms were copying the guidance plan. She wanted all educators in the preschool to read Gartrell's (2003) book, *The Power of Guidance*, to ensure they used the same strategy to manage the behavior of young boys in their classrooms. The director was instrumental in spreading the guidance plan strategy across the preschool and promoting consistent practice concerning behavior management among all educators.

Evidence suggested that NAEYC Standard 1: Promoting Child Development and Learning was increasingly met over the semester. Regarding Standard 1a: knowing and understanding the developmental and learning needs of each boy in the class, educators improved their developmentally-appropriate provision for boys' social, physical, language, and emotional needs, and increasingly understood the multiple influences on each boys' individual development and learning. Requirements for Standard 1b were increasingly met as educators appreciated the importance of forming close relationships with the boys, and supporting friendship between them.

Educators' improved understanding of the implementation of the guidance plan, created healthier and more respectful learning opportunities for boys during free-play and circle times especially. Improved learning opportunities for boys were particularly supportive of Standard 1c and of candidates' teaching during

Practicum. The impact of the action research enabled the teacher candidate to successfully implement four activities required in Practicum that were specifically planned to support and challenge each boys' learning and development. This level of professional action was only possible in a classroom in which NAEYC Standards (2009) were aligned with college teaching and was supportive of boys' all round developmental and learning needs.

Final Reflections

The aims of the action research were largely met. The guidance plan helped most educators develop beneficial interactions with boys, although some educators showed some resistance to changed practice. Communication skills among educators and boys were improved and boys' engagement in play was sustained. The teacher candidate was provided with regular opportunities during Practicum that made connections between NAEYC standards, taught in college classes, and educators' practice in Practicum. The teacher candidate enjoyed improved opportunities to design and implement lesson plan assignments aligned with NAEYC Standards (2009).

7. IMPROVING DIFFERENTIATION DURING MORNING MEETINGS

Teaching Challenge

Children's individual learning needs are not met during morning meeting times.

Background

Strategy: Using active games, visual aids, finger rhymes, and songs to differentiate activity.

The Context: The action research took place over one complete semester in a Pre-K classroom in a non-public elementary school. Full-day sessions were offered in a mixed-ability class that included children with diverse learning needs. There were 14 children in the class with a certified teacher and assistant teacher. The whole school including the Pre-K classroom used the Responsive Curriculum teaching approach.

Findings

1. An open-ended game enabled children to be a king and make up a rule of their own, and enabled their individual learning needs to be met.
2. Flexible wait times in games reflected children's individual abilities, and resulted in their individual learning needs being met.
3. Incorporating games that allowed movement helped meet children's individual learning needs with regard to timing, attention span, and developmental-appropriateness of their activity.

4. Finger rhymes enabled children to solve mathematical problems in individual ways.
5. Finger rhymes, where teachers asked differentiated questions, enabled children to supply different, but acceptable, answers.
6. Open-ended and active treasure-hunt games enabled children's individual learning needs to be met.
7. The use of games, visual aids, finger rhymes, songs and Sign Language resulted in the teacher and assistant teacher sharing the workload. One led the activity while the other recorded observations. The observations were used to plan subsequent differentiated lessons to meet children's individual learning needs.
8. Cards with single digits on them enabled teachers to differentiate mathematical concepts that matched individual children's understanding.

Summary

Whole-group, educator-led morning meetings failed to provide for each child's individual learning needs to be met. As a result, children were often restless and not learning. The inclusion of active games, visual aids, finger rhymes and songs enabled activities to be more open-ended and differentiated. Children's increased engagement during morning meetings gave educators time to observe their learning responses. Educators' changed teaching roles resulted in the assistant teacher recording daily observations of children's responses. The lead teacher used the observations to plan next-step, differentiated activities that accurately provided developmentally appropriate activities that supported each child's individual learning needs and improved their engagement.

The Teaching Challenge

Educators identified their teaching challenge as failing to provide sufficient diversity and inclusion during morning meeting. They described the difficulty in meeting children's diverse learning needs and ensuring they were all included during a large group time. Morning meeting typically consisted of a story, letter of the day, literacy and number activities. The team listed four difficulties connected to diversity and inclusion of each child during morning meeting.

First, teaching a mixed-ability class during whole group times was daunting. Educators tended to respond to more able children, i.e., those who volunteered answers, more than to those who did not. The educators' goal was to include all children in their teaching, regardless of ability and not leave any children out. However, teaching to children's diverse learning needs required different approaches which made the process very difficult. For some children, sequencing events in a story created a challenge for them. Others could not recognize a rhyme or the beginning letters of words, but for others, this material was too easy. Some children lacked social skills and were inattentive. Others were physically fidgety or simply unable to remain still at all. Some were

Fig 7.1: Individual learning needs were not met during morning meeting

less mature and this created a problem finding teaching material that was appropriate for each of them. Other children appeared to come from homes where learning was not highly valued, and so those children tended not to reflect school values.

Second, promoting inclusion in the classroom was difficult. Educators wondered how they could better include all children in lessons, a requirement at the time of the "No Child Left Behind" Act. Since the act required that all children, regardless of their abilities, be included in activities, educators were compelled to provide all children with opportunities to learn the same content. Educators' dilemma lay in the near impossibility of this, given the starkly diverse learning needs of the children in the class. Complicating this, no Individual Education Plans existed to alert educators to what children's special learning needs were. During morning meeting, educators asked administrators how they could better include the children with special needs. However, finding a good fit between the content they had to teach and the needs of slower-paced learners persisted. Educators wanted less able children to be included, to be like their peers, and not feel different or embarrassed by their lower ability levels. Educators were hard-pressed to find a way to accomplish this.

Third, responding to children's inattentiveness was highly demanding and took the educators' focus off what they were trying to teach. Some children, although physically present, were "somewhere else mentally" during morning meeting. They daydreamed and did not pay attention to taught activities. Educators thought they had children's attention when they were all quiet, but this was not the case. In reality, when children did not understand material, they "zoned out."

Fourth, differentiating teaching material was a challenge because young children of mixed-abilities required different stimuli to hold their attention. Educators wondered how to differentiate material so that children's different learning needs could be met during circle time. This was important, given that some children would have to repeat Pre-K. When educators taught to one ability level, they felt they caused embarrassment to children of a lower ability level. They worried that the sharper children might giggle if the slower students wrote incorrect answers on their boards. Educators asked, "What do we do about children who work slowly and cause others to become restless? How do we get the whole group back on task?" Educators noticed that some children already suffered self-esteem problems and were afraid of embarrassing themselves. Younger and less able children actively resisted answering questions by saying to educators, "I didn't have my hand up. I'm not answering," which in itself showed a level of awareness, implying that intellectual ability was there but not as easy for teachers to identify.

Team Values

Educators expressed their values about diversity and inclusion. Although educators wanted to accommodate diversity and meet children's individual learning needs, they felt the downward pressure of Kindergarten standards upon them. Educators remarked that Pre-K children had to meet those standards so they would not be behind when they entered kindergarten. Educators were willing to do extra work to compensate for any gaps in children's knowledge, and they recognized that they needed workable teaching strategies to help them meet children's diverse learning needs. They were genuinely irritated that they had not been taught these strategies, specifically in the areas of math and English Language Arts. Educators were worried about the ethical problems that could arise by teaching and treating all children the same. Children's diverse learning needs required diverse teaching approaches. Educators were ambivalent, because they offered some children 1:1 support, recognizing that not all children were the same. However, educators provided children with additional support in an attempt to prevent them from falling behind.

Aims of the Action Research

The following aims were identified to help educators: (1) use varied teaching approaches to meet the diverse learning needs of each child in a mixed ability class; (2) promote greater inclusion of every child during morning meeting; (3) increase every child's attentiveness during morning meeting; (4) differentiate material to better support each child's diverse learning needs; (5) align educators' practice more closely with NAEYC Standards (2009) regarding diversity and inclusion; and (6) improve teacher candidates' opportunities to complete Practicum assignments that aligned with those NAEYC Standards.

Alignment of Teaching Challenge with NAEYC Standards

The importance of teaching in ways that promoted diversity and inclusion was emphasized and integrated throughout all NAEYC Standards (2009). The commitment to diversity and inclusion was to ensure that the developmental and learning needs of each and every child were fully supported in the preschool classroom. Learning was more likely to be successful, and inequalities that might have led to persistent attainment gaps were minimized. Developmental and learning needs *can* include children with delays, disabilities, gifted and talented, cultural and linguistic diversity, socio-economic diversity, and individual learning-style preferences. The following standards respond to these learning needs: NAEYC Standard 1: Promoting Child Development and Learning, where teacher candidates show they use developmental knowledge to create healthy, respectful, supportive, and challenging learning environments for young children. Standard 3: Observing, Documenting and Assessing to Support Young Children and Families, teacher candidates practice responsible assessment, to promote outcomes for each child and Standard 5: Using Content Knowledge to Build Meaningful Curriculum, teacher candidates use their own knowledge, appropriate early learning standards, and other resources to design, implement and evaluate meaningful challenging curricula for each child, specifically in language, literacy, and mathematics.

Baseline Assessment

A 20-minute video was recorded to form a baseline assessment of the teaching challenge. A checklist of identified teaching challenges was devised by the team, and used to record the frequency of these challenges seen in the video:

Teaching Challenges	Frequencies
Children's inattentiveness	27
Teaching to children's individual diverse needs	5
Inclusive practices exist in activity	0

Table 7.1: Baseline assessment of the teaching challenge

A total of 32 examples were observed in two categories related to diversity, and inclusion during morning meeting. The most common category was children's inattentiveness (27) that manifested as children moved around and disrupted the flow of teaching. Six children moved to put sweaters in their cubbies, and three others moved to get tissues to wipe their noses. The seating arrangement, where children sat on the floor facing the teacher, perched on a high stool, compelled several of them to repeatedly turn around to see who was behind them. As children sat listening to letter and sound recognition work, individual children, selected by the teacher, did directed tasks, e.g., writing a beginning letter on the white board. At this point, several boys wriggled backwards and forward to move to another space to sit with other children. Others sat on their haunches, rocked from side to side, and used their arms to stabilize their weight. Some children talked to their neighbors. Some girls stroked their friends' hair and played with hair accessories. Others shuffled on their bottoms and played with trainer shoelaces.

Five activities were differentiated to meet children's diverse learning needs. The teacher wrote a morning message to the class that consisted of the day of the week, and the name of the class leader. The message illustrated the use of capital letters and the meaning of written text.

Selected children were individually asked to answer questions at various levels of difficulty, or asked to carry out prescribed tasks. Educators asked all children in the class to indicate whether they agreed or disagreed with particular concepts by giving a thumbs-up or thumbs down.

There were no examples of inclusive practices that enabled all children to participate in activities in different ways. The consistent format for writing the same morning message meant that content focused on classroom organization and prescribed letters of the week. Considerable "wait" time existed, because only one or two children actively participated during morning meeting. The rest of the class waited and became restless.

Team Reflection

The team identified three teaching problems. First, children's inattentiveness, resulted in learning deficits. Educators deduced that children's inattentiveness was not behavioral. Rather, they believed the teaching pace did not match children's individual learning needs, and was, therefore, problematic. Some children were inattentive because they were bored, others had lost track of the lesson and several wanted to participate even if they did not know the answers to questions. Educators questioned the developmental appropriateness of their teaching Pre-K children.

Second, educators recognized that their teaching was not differentiated because no system of assessment existed to identify each child's diverse learning needs. As a result, educators could not plan their teaching according to each child's diverse developmental levels. Instead, the Responsive Classroom curriculum imposed a daily routine on the classroom in which the teaching of letters and numbers was embedded. Educators were aware that when they asked children "closed" questions that required only "right" answers, the needs of more able children's individual learning needs were met. At the same time though, the needs of less-able children were ignored.

Third, educators said they wanted to use inclusive practices, but were unable to because no child had yet been diagnosed with special educational needs, and their specific learning needs were not immediately apparent to educators. By "inclusive practices" in their classroom, educators meant that their teaching should fit and challenge each child's current development and learning ability. The formal assessment made this difficult.

Selected Literature

The teacher candidates and the college librarian used a range of key words connected to the teaching challenge to find relevant journal articles. The teacher candidate selected the following articles for the team to read:

(1) Jalongo, M.R. (1996). Teaching young children to become better listeners. *Young Children* 51 (2): 21-26.

(2) McVicker, C.J. (2007). Young readers respond: The importance of child participation in emerging literacy. *Young Children* 62 (3): 18-22.

(3) Roskos, K.A. Christie J.F, & Richgels D.J. (2003). The essentials of early literacy instruction. *Young Children* 58 (2): 52-60. Online: www.journal.naeyc.org/btj/20030.

(4) Torbert, M. (2005). Using active group games to develop basic life skills. *Young Children* 60 (4): 72-78.

Since the teaching challenge incorporated a number of teaching elements, the team thought that combining a number of strategies, rather than using just one, would have greater impact. The team chose to implement three strategies from two articles: (1) Use a repertoire of active teaching approaches during morning meeting that included games, visual aids, finger rhymes, and songs to increase children's attentiveness (Torbert, 2005); (2) interact with children in reassuring ways to promote inclusion (Jalongo, 1996), and; (3) assess each child's understanding of concepts taught and use assessment outcomes to plan differentiated activities (Jalongo, 1996).

The strategies were checked for their developmental-appropriateness in Wood (2007) which said:

> ...4-year-olds learn best through varied approaches that include being read to, acting out stories, fairy tales, and manipulating math materials. Teachers need to focus on observing behavior and asking questions that lead children toward the next level of cognitive exploration and understanding (p31). Inclusion is best promoted by the lead teacher acting as primary care-giver who remains with her group of children for most of the day (p13).

Creating an Assessment Tool

The completed assessment grid seen at table 7.2 was used each time the team viewed strategy implementation videos. The purpose of the assessment grid was twofold. First, identify desirable outcomes of strategies; and second, observe and monitor the impact of strategies on the teaching challenge.

Video 1: Implementing Strategies

To promote desirable changes to their teaching during morning meeting, the team wanted to implement all three strategies as soon as possible. To increase children's attentiveness, they chose to use a wider repertoire of active teaching approaches than they had before. Games, visual aids, finger rhymes, and songs were included. After one week's implementation, the following frequencies were observed and recorded during a 20-minute video of morning meeting.

Fig 7.2: Child leading the game,
"If I were a king"

Assessment Criteria	Frequency	Comments
Inclusion is promoted	6	
Teaching is differentiated	0	
Children learn literacy knowledge	10	
Children learn mathematical knowledge	5	
Visual aids support attentiveness	2	
Finger rhymes support attentiveness	0	
Songs support attentiveness	0	

Assessment Criteria	Frequency	Comments
Games support attentiveness	5	

Table 7.2: Impact of active games on teaching

Team reflection after each video is viewed:

- Is the strategy working? How?
- Is the original teaching challenge being improved upon? How?
- Is children's learning improving? How?
- Is your understanding of your teaching changing? How?
- Is your teaching changing? How?
- What do we do next in our teaching? How?

Twenty-eight frequencies were recorded to show the impact of using active games during morning meeting to promote diversity and inclusion. During this video, the use of other strategies–finger rhymes and songs–was not included. Three games were used: (1) if I were a king; (2) matching picture cards and initial letter cards; and (3) a treasure hunt. Three examples of using visual aides were observed that included: (1) a crown; (2) picture cards with corresponding letter cards; and (3) number cards.

All children were fully attentive on six extended occasions when they participated in three games. In the first game, six children, one at a time, pretended to be a king by wearing a crown and said what they would do if they were king for a day. This literacy game was open-ended, and children were encouraged to say whatever they wanted. As a result, educators did not need to ask differentiated questions.

In the second game, ten examples of children learning the letter "k" for king were recorded. In this game beginning letters and sounds were emphasized. In pairs, children matched a picture card of an object, e.g., an apple to the corresponding initial letter card "a."

In another game, children were asked whether the two picture cards they drew out of a kangaroo's pouch had the same starting sound, e.g., banana and bird, yes, and kangaroo and mittens, no.

In the third game, five examples were observed of children playing a number game in which they were asked to hunt in the room and find examples of numbers that were less than five and more than six.

These literacy and number games resulted in all children being fully attentive, which suggested that diversity and inclusion were effectively promoted through active games, open-ended questioning, and exploration of numbers.

Team Reflection

Educators evaluated that overall the strategy of using games with visual aids during morning meeting was successful in increasing children's attentiveness. As a result, diversity and inclusion were effectively promoted. The assistant educator said that she saw, "good things, and that certain children had surprised her with really good answers, for example, one king said he would make sure that all children were happy and there would be no war."

Regarding the use of visual aids, educators noticed that children's concentration was improved when they reached into containers and acted with materials. Children were interested in comparing the picture cards to see if the pictures started with the same sound. However, passing just one kangaroo's pouch around the whole class for children to choose letter cards from resulted in them having to wait for their turn and some became restless.

The original teaching challenge was improved upon because the video showed how children were attentive when they were able to participate in games and visual aids.

With children's increased attentiveness in place, the assistant educator had time to start implementing the third strategy, concerned with assessing what each child understood during morning meeting. The assistant educator commented on how, as an observer, she was able to see more of what children did. However, the use of K-W-L assessment charts, (what I know, what I want to know and what I learned) used in the Responsive Curriculum, was not an assessment method that provided information on each child's learning.

As an alternative, the teacher candidate suggested recording anecdotal observations of each child during morning meetings. She had learned this assessment method in college courses, and it was deemed appropriate, because it would provide information about each child's individual learning progress.

The assistant educator wrote down daily observations on five children during morning meeting. She shared the observations with the lead educator who used them to assess each child's understanding, and to plan related challenging activities for the next morning meeting. Educators took on new professional roles as they worked collaboratively to gather evidence about every child's learning, and assess the impact of the strategies. Educators preferred to observe children because observations showed how each child's mind worked and reacted to activities (see fig.7.3).

The team reported how writing down anecdotal observations enabled them to understand how children used mathematical calculations to come up with answers, e.g., when the educator said "Show me eight fingers. Eight children went swimming. Two got cold and got out of the pool. How many children were left in the pool?" A child answered by holding up fingers, and saying, 5 + 1 (rather than 6). Educators realized that many Pre-K children were not yet able to use the mathematical skills of adding fingers on two hands together. Observations at figure 7.3 showed educators how many children did not understand the literacy and math concepts embedded in games and visual aids. Educators found that their teaching had to respond to children's *current* conceptual understanding before children's further learning could take place.

Regarding the impact of the strategy to promote inclusion, the assistant educator commented that children did not like the lead educator sitting on the floor as it was difficult for them to see her and to follow finger rhymes. As a result, the lead educator sat on a low chair that enabled her to be more visible to the children but remain close to them. Children responded with more patience when they were told that everyone would get a turn either today, or tomorrow. Educators commented they were developing more reasonable expectations about children's attentiveness. It was not reasonable to expect 100% attentiveness during morning meeting, but it was reasonable to expect most children to be attentive most of the time. The team reflected they would no longer see their teaching as a failure if all children were not attentive 100% of the time.

One educator said: "If there's too much of a wait, he can't stay focused. He's fast and he must not be sidetracked by waiting. We have to adapt our teaching so that his wait time is not too long." This finding was an important indicator regarding how educators taught. Rather than thinking that children caused challenges to their teaching, educators realized their approach needed to change. The team decided to continue implement-

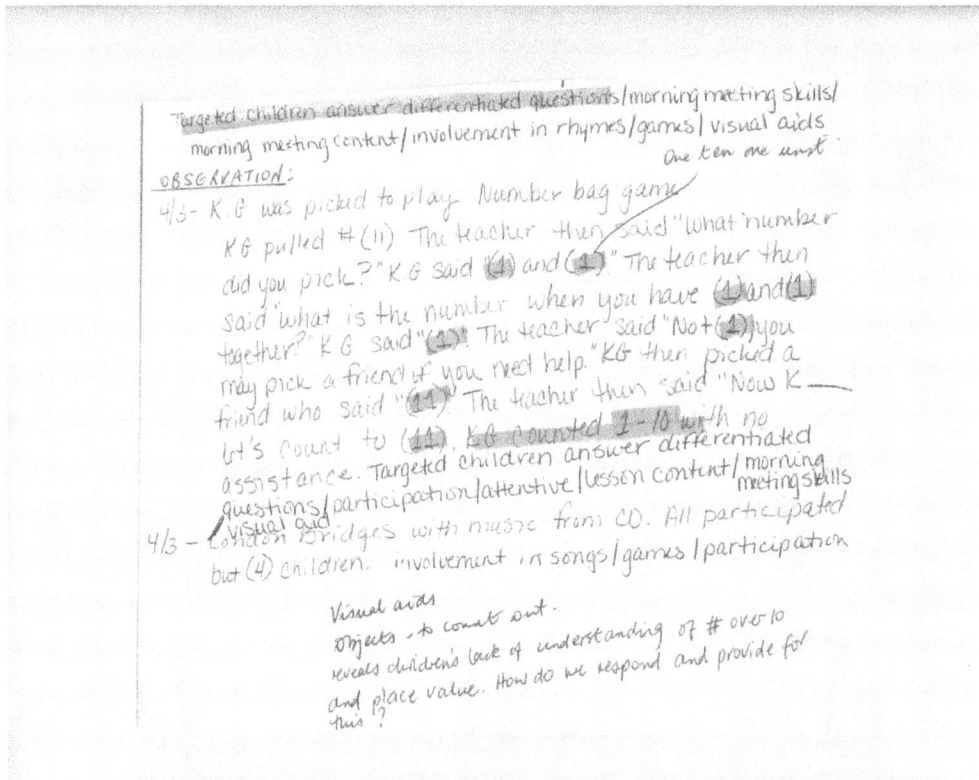

Targeted children answer differentiated questions/morning meeting skills/
morning meeting content/ involvement in rhymes/games/ visual aids
one ten one unit

OBSERVATION:
4/3 - K.G was picked to play Number bag game.
K.G pulled #(11) The teacher then said "what number
did you pick?" K.G said (1) and (1)." The teacher then
said "what is the number when you have (1) and (1)
together?" K.G said "(1)." The teacher said "No + (1) you
may pick a friend if you need help." K.G then picked a
friend who said "(11)" The teacher then said "Now K___
let's count to (11). K.G counted 1-10 with no
assistance. Targeted children answer differentiated
questions/participation/attentive/lesson content/morning meeting skills
4/3 - London Bridges with music from CD. All participated
but (4) children. involvement in songs/games/participation

Visual aids
Objects + to count out.
reveals children's lack of understanding of # over 10
and place value. How do we respond and provide for
this?

Fig. 7.3: An educator's observation of child's mathematical understanding

ing their increased repertoire of teaching approaches, and further develop differentiated planning to meet each child's diverse needs.

Fig 7.4: Children play alphabet game matching a picture to an initial sound card

Assessment Criteria	Frequency	Comments
Children are attentive	7	
Targeted children answer differentiated questions	7	
Children learn letters	3	
Children learn numbers	2	
Visual aids support involvement	4	
Finger rhymes support involvement	7	
Songs support involvement	1	
Games support involvement	1	

Table 7.3: Impact of using finger rhymes and games

When educators used more active games and finger rhymes during morning meeting, they recorded a total of 35 frequencies. This was an increase from the number of frequencies observed in the first video. On seven occasions, all children were fully attentive, and inclusion was promoted as they simultaneously acted out with their hands and sang the finger rhyme, "Itsy Bitsy Spider." Children laughed as they sang, made noises and copied the teacher's hand movements signifying "down came the rain and washed the spider out." The teacher asked differentiated and open-ended questions about the spider that enabled three children of different abilities to give three different but acceptable answers. In contrast with the first video, there was a 7-fold increase in the frequency of differentiation.

The teacher asked children to consider the letter E during the finger rhyme. In pairs, children went on a treasure hunt around the room to find the letter, E. Children found the letter printed on shoes, on shape posters in the word square and hexagon, and in children's names written on the front of drawers. The concept of searching out the letter E was continued as one child at a time wore "elephant's ears." In conclusion, the teacher extended vocabulary work by exploring the word, "enormous." The teacher asked for three different definitions of the word that enabled three children to participate by using different examples. The frequency of children learning letters decreased from the first video (from 10 to 3). The drop was explained by activities being more active and better understood by children, but they took up more time.

The number of the week was 7 and was explored as children counted to seven. The concept of larger and smaller numbers was explored as children picked number tiles out of a bag and said whether they were less than, or greater than, the number 7. Visual aids in the form of elephant's ears and a bag of number tiles supplemented the teaching on four occasions. More frequencies in the use of finger rhymes (7), songs (1), and games (1) were observed in the second video than the first.

Team Reflection

The team reported that the implementation of the strategy using more active games, finger rhymes, and songs improved children's attentiveness. Using finger play was found to be particularly effective, e.g., while reading Zinnia's Flower Garden, by Monica Wellington, children role-played planting rows of seeds with their fingers.

During finger play, children were more active and not as fidgety. As a result, their participation and attentiveness increased.

Educators reported not having to intervene over inattentiveness as much during morning meeting. The assistant educator said, "I am a distraction. They don't need me as much, and I now stay back and can spend more time observing."

The lead educator identified her improved time management skills as a factor in children's improved attentiveness. She now organized morning meeting into three blocks of activity focused on language, literacy, and mathematics, and used her wider repertoire of teaching approaches in all three blocks. She judged children's attention spans and pace of learning more accurately by understanding that it was not possible for all children to have a turn during each morning meeting. Instead, she encouraged children to play in small groups and asked them to communicate with each other, rather than with her directly. Incorporating playful games, rhymes, and visual aids, activities had resulted in the children being more attentive, and had increased the ways they learned letters and numbers. In the short term, the use of a wider repertoire of teaching approaches had created more preparation work for educators, but at the same time, was creating a bank of activities that educators would use again.

One positive outcome of the strategy of using games, rhymes, visual aids, and activities was that learning had become more social and the classroom was more inclusive. Activities frequently involved children working with partners and teaching things to each other. Working in small groups and in pairs resulted in children and educators changing roles. When one group finished an activity before another, children tended to help each other. Children were occupied doing things and learned more actively than when they were expected to sit and listen.

Educators identified movement as another positive outcome of the strategies. Movement was said to help children learn, focus their attention, and communicate together. Movement during songs and games provided opportunities for target children (who were observed in need of more help) to be involved in activities. The assistant teacher said she had "been blown out of the water" by children's responsiveness in number games. For example, making patterns with number cards when children stood in a line making a repeated pattern by holding up the numbers 1,1; 8,8; 1,1; 8,8.

The team reported how they had developed a professional partnership resulting from the assistant educator recording observations of five children's learning during morning meeting each day. The lead teacher and the assistant teacher used the observations to assess the five children's understanding of concepts taught each day, and also planned differentiated learning activities for the five children for the next day.

Educators enjoyed the partnership and the open-minded approach to teaching that had developed. They liked the way that, as one participant said, "it's all coming from the children." The assistant educator's role of recording observations gave the lead teacher accurate information about each child's attainment. As a result, she understood current learning needs, and was able to plan differentiated activities for those children. These activities included asking specific questions built on what they had already done, and more open-ended questions that had many right answers, rather than just one. Instead of educators using the Responsive Curriculum routine to drive morning meetings, educators now used each child's individual observations as an indicator of their current learning needs.

The team decided to continue with differentiating activities during the final stage of the project.

Using Games to Increase Differentiation

Assessment Criteria	Frequency	Comments
Children are attentive	9	On 9 occasions
Targeted children answer differentiated questions	5	Five children were asked questions based on yesterday's anecdotes
Children learn letters	2	Not clear why particular letters have been chosen – q, z
Children learn numbers	2	Why 1 and 8? Note 1+8=18
Visual aids support involvement	4	Children like the sun. We could have many suns to promote more involvement
Finger rhymes support involvement	0	
Songs support involvement	1	
Games support involvement	1	

Table 7.4: impact of and inclusion differentiated activities on attentiveness

Twenty-four frequencies were recorded on video. Children were observed to be attentive and inclusion was promoted on nine occasions. This was the highest recorded frequency of attentiveness throughout the action research and was judged to have resulted from the planning of differentiated and open-ended activities during morning meeting. Children were attentive as they were asked to think of words that begin with QU and Z. They said the words quiet, quick, zebra, zany and zig-zag. When exploring the letter S, children were invited to hold a visual aid of the sun and were asked an open-ended question about what they enjoyed doing on a sunny day. One child participated by saying that she would ride her bike and another said she would play outside.

Children were asked to pick out number cards with either number 1 or 8 written on them. Children were then asked to find a partner so they could make up the number 18. Children were asked what number came first in 18, 1 (representing ten) or 8. Then children were asked to find the two number cards that made up number 18 and hold these cards up in front of them. The activity concluded with children being asked addition and subtraction operations using numbers 1 and 8. Children's addition answers $1 + 8 = 18$ and $1 + 8 = 9$ and subtraction answers $8 - 1 = 7$ and $8 - 1 = 5$ indicated their current number fluency and what aspects of teaching needed adjustment to suit each child.

Team Reflection

The strategy was deemed to be working. In particular, when the team asked children more open-ended questions they were more attentive.

The original teaching challenge was improved upon when children were given more latitude in their thinking. They were able to contribute more freely to discussions.

However, some children were reluctant to speak in front of the whole class.

Previously, educators thought these children were embarrassed, but now they wondered whether their reluctance was explained by lack of understanding.

Educators thought about ways to increase each child's participation and encouraged them to speak in pairs. The benefits of this were attentiveness, increased inclusion and the elimination of wait time. All children in the class participated in discussions at the same time. Educators could observe what children said and assess their understanding.

The concept of using numbers in activities was discussed and made more relevant to children, e.g., a child's birthday or the number of a child's house, was introduced. Educators also considered it more developmentally appropriate if numbers were restricted to fewer than ten, because place value was too abstract a concept for most Pre-K children to understand.

The video revealed the importance of educators' teaching each mathematical concept by using context and consistent language. This was to avoid confusion to children when teaching conservation of number, i.e., place-value pattern, addition, subtraction, and numbers less than and greater than.

Educators recognized the importance for focused plans by making sure that concepts were connected. They thought it was best to differentiate teaching by using observations recorded by the assistant teacher that indicated children's individual learning outcomes from the previous day, and to focus on one concept at a time. To make children's mathematical operations more concrete, the team decided that manipulative materials, e.g., cubes, bears and tiles would be used during morning meeting.

Final Reflection

The team determined that the aims of the action research were met. A more varied repertoire of active teaching approaches had helped to meet the diverse learning needs of each child in class. Inclusion of every child had been promoted during morning meeting by increasing social interaction among children, and between children and educators. Each child's attentiveness had been increased during morning meeting. Each child's diverse learning needs were better supported by differentiating material that was made possible by the introduction of a system of observation.

Educators' practice was more closely aligned with NAEYC Standards (2009) regarding diversity and inclusion. Standard 5: Using Content Knowledge to Build Meaningful Curriculum was the first standard to be better aligned. A wider repertoire of active learning approaches used during morning meeting resulted in the design, implementation, and evaluation of challenging curricula for each child. This was specifically in the content areas of language, literacy, and mathematics. Standard 3: Observing, Documenting, and Assessing to Support Young Children and Families was better aligned through the introduction of a responsible assessment method. The recording of daily anecdotal observations on five or more different children enabled educators to assess those children's current attainment and plan the next day's activities in ways that promoted appropriate outcomes for each child.

NAEYC Standard 1: Promoting Child Development and Learning was aligned and enabled the teacher candidate to show she used developmental knowledge to create healthy, respectful, supportive, and challenging learning environments for young children. Strong evidence also existed for alignment with Standard 6: Becoming a Professional. The ELC team enabled alignment with Standards 6b and 6c: concerning engaging in collaborative learning and integrating knowledgeable, reflective and critical perspectives on early education to be met. This was particularly supportive of the teacher candidate writing and implementing Practicum assignments that aligned with what was taught in college.

The team evaluated that the three strategies, when used together, had been successful in improving the original teaching challenge for diversity and inclusion. The prospect of teaching a diverse class during whole group times was no longer daunting. Using a repertoire of active games, finger rhymes, visual aids, and songs, effectively promoted children's attentiveness and inclusion.

The strategy of sitting closely to children and letting them know they will all have a turn allows the children to be more relaxed. Educators thought their own "in the moment" developmentally-appropriate interactions with young children had successfully promoted inclusion. Children were more social and physically active, and as a result, classroom community was better developed.

The use of responsible assessment meant educators spent less time "policing" children and more time analyzing children's learning needs. Observations had made it possible for educators to know what each child understood and to prepare differentiated activities for the next day that closely fit each child's learning needs. The possibility existed to ask particular children "closed" questions that assumed different levels of ability and also met their individual learning needs.

Educators' values changed as a result of the action research. The reading of professional articles resulted in their being more knowledgeable about teaching strategies. These strategies improved their teaching and helped them overcome their ethical concerns about diversity and inclusion. Educators became less concerned about the pressure of Kindergarten standards, and instead were more concerned with using developmentally-appropriate content and materials for the children in their Pre-K class. The increased use of a repertoire of active teaching approaches resulted in a more developmentally-appropriate Pre-K curriculum. It enabled educators to enjoy the current stage of learning and not be concerned about the next. Educators' fears about children being embarrassed as they participated in activities were reduced. A built-in system of assessment that addressed diverse learning needs, enabled educators to plan differentiated activities for each child, both in small groups and in paired activities.

Educators acknowledged that their action research was not complete. However, the teacher candidate had fully contributed to the action research throughout the semester. She was able to act on the improved congruency between NAEYC Standards, the teaching in college, and the implementation of course assignments in the Practicum classroom.

PART III: REFLECTIONS

8. PARTICIPANTS' RESPONSES TO THE ELC

Purpose

The purpose of this chapter is to: (1) report and discuss participants' questionnaire responses to the ELC; and (2) discuss and evaluate the strengths and weaknesses of the ELC as an early childhood professional development model.

Data Collection Methods

At the end of each semester, team participants completed questionnaires on the ELC. These questionnaires are seen at Appendix A (Educators' questionnaire) and Appendix B (Teacher Candidates' questionnaire). While self-reported questionnaire responses must be approached with caution, they do indicate how participants responded to the ELC at the end of their action research semester. A largely qualitative approach was used to analyze the 25 questionnaire responses in the six case studies featured in this book. The participants comprised six teachers, six teachers' assistants, six teacher candidates, and three team leaders. Some questions included a numerical scale that comprised five levels of response. These questions were analyzed quantitatively and reported in percentage terms.

Data from questionnaires were combined to reveal participants' responses to the ELC, and the impact it had on their professional development. Themes in data responses were organized into the following four categories: (1) professional attitudes; (2) professional relationships; (3) teaching skills, and; (4) inquiry skills.

Recurring patterns in each category are highlighted in **boldface** to draw readers' attention to them. The quantitative and qualitative findings in each category are reported in order of the strength of the finding. The implications of participants' responses are discussed and used to evaluate the ELC as a model of early childhood professional development. The implications of participants' responses are used to make recommendations for improved and aligned practice in early childhood preschool settings, and in teacher education programs.

Questionnaire Findings

(1) Professional attitudes

Participants rated the development of professional attitudes as either *positive* or *very positive*, suggesting that professional attitudes are effectively developed in the ELC.

Participants	Very positive	Positive
Teachers	33%	66%
Teacher Assistants	33%	66%
Teacher Candidates	100%	0%
Team Leaders	80%	20%

Table: 8.1: Rankings concerning the development of professional attitudes

Professional attitudes were developed through increased **motivation** and increased **enlightenment**.

Motivation

Participants' reported increased **motivation** to overcome the teaching challenges they faced. New strategies introduced into classrooms put them in greater control of their teaching so they were no longer left to take care of challenges on their own. Teacher assistants reported how action research enabled them to see how new strategies worked. They had to keep learning new things to improve their practice. One teacher assistant explained how her increased motivation created "a calmer and more comfortable classroom environment." Her job was easier when she spent less time dealing with behavioral problems.

Participants reported how increased motivation affected their **job satisfaction.** Greater use of child-centered teaching approaches gave children more ownership of their own learning. Enabling children to make choices and decisions helped educators better understand each child's exact learning needs. One teacher said she had "a new appreciation of what children brought into the classroom," and this enabled her to base her teaching on the capabilities of each child. Teachers and teacher assistants reported being more proactive with increased job satisfaction. Asking children questions that were directly related to their play enabled educators to engage more purposefully and sustain the play longer. However, unfavorable employment conditions discouraged some teachers from being proactive. Low pay rates, lack of recognition, and high stress levels deterred them from improving their practice. Other teacher-aides reported how challenging it was to use new teaching strategies because "it required (them) to think in new ways they were not used to."

Problem-solving increased participants' motivation. When teams identified their own teaching challenge, their participation in action research increased. Educators solved problems through more creative use of resources and through better interaction with children. Teachers commented how working in the ELC was a "great experience because they had developed positive attitudes towards problem-solving that affected how children learned." One teacher commented, "I was more excited and more confident about my work. I wanted to find out if I could make things better." For example, differentiating activities was found to increase children's inclusion in activities and resulted in more meaningful play opportunities. However, some teacher candidates expressed concern about poor provision for boys. Because "boys rarely stood still," problem-solving to improve physical provision was reported as crucial for an effective classroom.

Enlightenment

Participants were more **enlightened** about their practice and this affected their professional attitudes. Partnerships between teacher and teacher's aide in classrooms promoted enlightenment. Instead of working on tasks often related to "crowd control, snacks, and toilet times," teacher assistants' practice was developed when they took on new classroom roles. Teacher assistants' written observations were used to assess children's learning and enabled the planning of next-step activities. Partnerships helped teacher assistants "know how to iron-out teaching problems that resulted in calmer routines for children and for educators." However, some educators did not show the same level of enlightenment and showed resistance to making changes to their teaching.

Team meetings enabled teacher candidates to become more enlightened about their classrooms. Using child-centered teaching approaches enabled teacher candidates to be more responsive and respectful of children. Teacher candidates expected to observe in Practicum classrooms, and to teach their lesson plan assignments, but they did not expect to take on new roles required in the ELC related to overcoming teaching problems. Team leaders reported how new partnerships were formed among **different early childhood classrooms and agencies** involved in Practicum. The sharing and disseminating of improved teaching practices at end-of-semester conferences were particularly important. Results spread among a diverse audience of early childhood agencies promoted change, not just in one agency, but "across the board.".

Discussion of professional attitudes

Overall, professional attitudes were positively affected. The mixing of professional theory and practice changed professional actions in classrooms (Moyles, J. 2001, Thornton, J.S., Crim, C.L. & Hawkins, J., 2009). This was important for three reasons: (1) When educators undertook professional development in teams, they learned about theory together, and applied it consistently in their classrooms. (2) Educators' theoretical understanding and professional practice were identified as the starting points for intervention (Harwood, Klopper, Oshanyin & Vanderlee, 2013). This ensured that new strategies were built into educators' existing early childhood knowledge and prevented gaps and assumptions from developing. (3) New strategies that promoted new professional actions had an impact on educators' roles and the learning opportunities they made available to children (Christ & Wang, 2013). Resistance to new practices shown by some educators suggested that changed practice was developmental and more likely to be achieved through professional development that took place over time (Engstrom, M.E. & Danielson, L. M,2006, Roehhig, Dubosarsky, Mason, Carlson & Murphy, 2011).

Educators' self-reliance enabled them to work effectively in teams in their own classrooms, and not rely on input from outsiders (Stremmel, 2002). Despite increased requirements, and calls for more accountability, educators showed they could be trusted and were responsible for their own professional development to promote improved teaching (Helterbran & Fennimore, 2004).

Providing for both children's care and their learning needs was found to be at the heart of an improved early childhood curriculum. This contrasts to a current emphasis on teaching to learning standards and demonstrating outcomes. Although learning standards are often used to improve the quality of what children experience in the classroom, they can risk hyper-standardization of the curriculum that is insensitive to the needs of each child. Instead of improving provision, learning standards can inadvertently narrow what children experience in classrooms (Meisels, 2011). The elevation of educators' roles to incorporate observation, assessment, and planning, released some of them from routine jobs. (Jones, Ratcliff, Sheehan, & Hunt 2012).

Unfortunately, poor employment conditions undermined some educators' motivation. Until greater value is placed on the work that educators do and reflected in improved employment conditions, the impact of professional development may not improve outcomes for children as intended (Moloney, 2010; Whitebook, M., 2014).

The new role of **problem-solvers** transformed educators' professional attitudes. Concerns in five out of six Practicum classrooms, about the poor learning experiences of boys, indicated the pervasiveness of certain teaching challenges. Therefore, if problem-solving is pertinent to improved teaching, the focus of professional development lies inside classrooms, rather than being imposed by outside agencies (Bruno, 2007). Educators' own classroom experiences show that they themselves have a critical role in setting professional development agendas that drive their new professional actions.

Working in teams was instrumental in the development of improved professional attitudes (Picchio, Giovannine, Mayer & Musatti, 2012). This suggests that defining educators' roles in teams, how they share and use information about children, and how their professional growth is supported, has to be more clearly articulated (Clark & Huber, 2005, Jones, et al., 2012). This is necessary to promote consistent and effective professional attitudes and practices among educators. However, until professional development is *routinely* made available to support educators, in varied early childhood agencies, the benefits of early childhood education for children may not be realized.

(2) Professional relationships developed in the ELC

Very positive, positive, or average rankings indicated in Table 8.2 suggested professional relationships were well-developed in the ELC.

Participant	Very positive	Positive	Average
Teachers	66%	17%	17%
Teacher Assistants	50%	50%	0%
Teacher Candidates	66%	17%	0%
Team Leaders	60%	40%	0%

Table 8.2: Participants' rankings for the development of professional relationships

Professional relationships were supported through team collaboration, interaction, understanding, responsibility, and time.

Team collaboration promoted strong professional relationships. Some 75% of participants said collaborative teamwork was the most important factor in promoting their professional relationships. One teacher reported, "Working in a team was a great experience because teachers were no longer left to cope with teaching challenges alone." Teacher assistants appreciated how teamwork enabled them to hear varied perspectives about teaching challenges. Sharing ideas led to more consistent teaching in classrooms. Teamwork was beneficial for teacher candidates. Their confidence grew through involvement in teams that resulted in closer partnerships between classrooms, the college, and across the local early childhood community. Teacher candidates brought new ideas to the team. However, working in teams was intimidating to some. Creating PowerPoint and iMovie presentations throughout the semester was found to be challenging.

Collaboration with administrators was crucial to effective professional relationships. With administrators' support, curriculum changes were implemented more easily and resources were more available. However, without administrators' support, educators could not easily make changes in classrooms. Because administrators' attendance at team meetings was not a requirement of the ELC, these individuals were not always aware of "remarkable" progress brought about in key curriculum areas. A lack of communication between administrators and some educators caused confusion over ELC expectations and resulted in some educators being unprepared for action research. Grant money paid to administrators to fund staff cover, and to purchase materials for action research, was interpreted as an incentive to participate. This meant that grant funding was not always used as intended.

Interaction between educators from different early childhood agencies enabled an exchange of ideas that resulted in new perspectives on practice. One educator mentioned how interaction reduced stress levels in classrooms. Interaction enabled teacher candidates to form professional relationships with educators and "fit right into the team." Teacher candidates felt more confident when asking educators questions about their professional practice. Respect for educators' knowledge and skills developed. Most educators interacted enthusiastically, were more open to strategies, and responsive to video findings. However, some educators were resistant to change in their teaching. This was not obvious until strategies were being implemented.

Interactions during team meetings led to improved **interactions in classrooms**. A sharing of knowledge among educators about children's needs made them more responsive to children. Teacher candidates were more insightful about how they interacted with children. Better relationships resulted from teacher candidates observing children in different play situations related to the action research. One teacher candidate said she was "more confident interacting with children" because she understood more about their development. Appropriate interactions resulted in children being more accepting of her than she had expected.

Professional Understanding

Action research strengthened professional relationships. Educators described action research as "a good way to learn," because their understanding of teaching young children was improved. One educator commented, "I am better at helping children learn because I spend less time sorting out behavior problems than before." Educators' improved understanding and related practice resulted in children's play being better supported. Children showed greater resilience, and were better equipped to sort out their own problems. Team discussions helped teacher candidates gain a deeper understanding of the classroom. Recording observations and watching video footage enabled them to see how young children learned and what their preferences were.

One teacher candidate commented how "observations opened her eyes to events that she would have missed otherwise." Her view of the children's capabilities evolved and she understood they were significantly more capable when given opportunities to do more. Teacher candidates were aware of the differences between children, and the complexity of creating an inclusive classroom in which each child's needs were provided for. One candidate remarked, "There is a lot to do concerning teaching each child and using new materials, making (teaching) much more demanding than I thought." Some teacher candidates noted that some educators' limited knowledge of child development hindered the action research.

Responsibility

Professional responsibility was fostered by feelings of "all of us being in this together." Shared responsibility was implemented when teams learned about the **interdependent variables** that affected the quality of their teaching. Educators singled out many teacher candidates for their diligence and willingness to learn about teaching. On the flip side, some teacher candidates showed weak time-management, resulting in some tasks being left unfinished at strategic times in the semester. Those teacher candidates were oblivious to the impact that their mismanagement had on the rest of the team, the impact on their own learning experiences and on the children's experiences.

Time

Release time from teaching was essential to the development of educators' professional relationships. It enabled the weekly hour-long team meetings to take place, which gave teams time to watch and analyze videos and plan their next action research moves.

While administrators provided release time for teachers to attend team meetings, teacher assistants were not always released. This did not necessarily defeat the purpose of the team meetings, but it did impact how consistently strategies were implemented. Although the weekly one-hour release time for team meetings was deemed a "great start," the hour was not sufficient time for teams to implement all aspects of the action research. One team leader commented, "One hour was not long enough for the team to fully reflect on what happened each week and to understand change at a deeper level."

Discussion of professional relationships

The ELC had positive effects on most participants' **professional relationships.** Good opportunities were created for educators to interact, thus improving professional understanding and practice. Professional development was particularly effective when teams from different early childhood agencies worked together (Messenger, 2013).

Teachers and teacher assistants in Practicum classrooms provided the starting point to build the professional development teams (Picchio, Giovannini, Mayer & Musatti, 2012). The addition of teacher candidates and team leaders created opportunities for other varied educators to participate in action research (Watson, R., & Wildy, H. 2014).

Teams called for a changed emphasis in teacher education programs. Instead of preparing teacher candidates to work as individuals during Practicum, a team approach was preferred, preparing them to work in such a way that teaching decisions and actions would be made in a social and collaborative context (Moyles, 2001). Assignments that required teacher candidates to work in teams, helped build professional knowledge, teaching actions, and professional relationships (Moran M.J. 2007). Teams helped teacher candidates to develop professional dispositions regarding the timely completion of assignments, and the understanding of the negative impact on the whole team when this progress was not made (McCann, E.J. & Turner, J.E. 2004; Kleyn, T., & Valle, J. 2014).

The participation of administrators was important to professional relationships (Albrecht, K. M. & Engel, B. 2007). Administrators were key decision makers, but because their involvement was *not* a requirement, few participated regularly.

Ideally, college faculty and administrators should communicate at the start of the ELC semester to agree on levels of participation, uses of funding, release of educators from teaching duties, and support strategies to improve teaching challenges. (Tomal, 2010).

Although implementing strategies, and making presentations supported educators' professional growth and relationships (Dickenson & Brady, 2006), some educators showed reluctance to changed practice. They often adapted strategies to reflect what they had already done. Some educators clung tenaciously to former teaching practices, rather than undergo the changes that would have required them to rethink their practice and work in new ways (Dickenson & Brady, 2006). These findings suggest that **change theory** is an important addition needed to action research which prepares educators to anticipate the difficulty of changing their practice.

Interaction between educators during team meetings improved how teacher candidates interacted with children in classrooms (Jalongo & Isenberg, 2000). Teacher candidates' growing knowledge and confidence enabled them to effectively relate to children in ways that better supported children's learning. This was evident as teacher candidates took on new practices that prepared them to provide for children's individual learning needs. The transfer of knowledge from team meetings to classroom practice suggested that teacher candidates' growth is a shared responsibility during Practicum and is not something teacher candidates should be expected to do alone.

One-hour weekly team meetings provided regular release time for teams to meet, but this was insufficient time to plan, carry out, and reflect on teaching changes as they happened (Whitington, Thompson & Shore, 2014). In addition, some teacher candidates' poor time management meant tasks were not completed on time. These findings suggested that sufficient time for professional development has to be provided during Practicum to: facilitate team meetings; foster professional interaction; ensure all aspects of the action research work is completed in the semester and develop teacher candidates' professional dispositions concerning the timely completion of tasks.

(3) Teaching skills developed in the ELC

Participants reported that the following teaching skills were developed: using child development knowledge; recording assessment; incorporating content area knowledge; and alignment with learning standards.

Child Development Knowledge

Very positive and *positive* rankings were recorded regarding the use of child development knowledge.

Participants	Very positive	Positive
Teachers	80%	20%
Teacher Assistants	60%	40%
Teacher Candidates	80%	20%
Team Leaders	80%	20%

Table 8.3: Participants' ratings for using child development

Most educators reported their use of child development knowledge was improved. Knowledge of 3- to 5-year-old **children's development**, and how to apply it in their teaching actions, was reinforced through reference books. The book, *Yardsticks*, was described as a "practical resource" that enabled educators to review the typical characteristics of 4-year-olds, and the factors that affected their development (Wood, 2007). Child development charts helped teams understand 4-year-olds' growth patterns, their capabilities, their curriculum needs, and how to incorporate these in their teaching. One teacher commented, "It is helpful to have **child devel-**

opment theory woven into the action research, because then we know that our actions are right for our children." One teacher candidate said, "I no longer guess how to approach my teaching. Instead, child development knowledge provided me with an accurate understanding of the needs of 4-year-olds, and what I have to include in my teaching during Practicum."

Improved child development knowledge strengthened educators' awareness of each child as an **individual learner.** Teams were reminded of how each child's individual learning needs were affected by their home background, ability, gender, socio-economic status, and culture. Well-developed observation skills were recognized as essential for educators to understand each child's individual needs, and especially so for younger children, and for those who came from diverse and disadvantaged backgrounds. One teacher candidate commented that, "The individual nature of each child's development means there is no 'best way' to teach all young children at the same time. Instead, I must understand each child's different developmental characteristics and modify activities so they promote each child's participation." Creating an inclusive classroom in which each individual child's needs were met was difficult. Several teacher assistants pointed out how a strong attachment to each child was essential in order to understand their developmental needs.

Developmental charts helped teams assess the suitability of teaching strategies as they related to children's needs. One team leader commented, "It was no good using a teaching strategy that was inappropriate for 4-year-olds, because we would end up with more problems than we started with." One teacher commented, "The impact of poverty and culture is 'huge' in my classroom. I have to consider these factors in how I teach." Teachers forged a match between children's age and stage of development, their general and individual learning needs, and the activities they made available to children. One team leader reported how knowledge of child development enabled educators to have better insights into what children did at particular stages of development. This meant their teaching was more "on target, and took account of individual development."

Teacher candidates' knowledge of **child development domains** ensured that content areas were taught appropriately. Including **literacy** across the curriculum helped build children's skills in speaking, listening, reading, and writing. Children's—and particularly boys'—**intellectual** growth in math, science, and social studies content areas were then supported. Children's **emotional development** was found to be supported by teaching content knowledge in literacy, science, and creative arts. This was identified as "huge for boys because it helped them cope and interact better with others in the classroom." Teaching content knowledge in ways that incorporated **physical development** enabled children's free movement which was found to have a positive impact on behavior. One candidate explained how "enabling children to move in activities allowed them to use their bodies to take their learning forward. At the same time, children stay calm."

Most educators said content knowledge was best taught in a **play-based** curriculum because this ensured the learning was exactly right for each child's development. A play-based curriculum required the provision of engaging **learning environments** that had well equipped play-centers for children to use. One teacher commented how "...grant funding had increased the range of physical equipment in the classroom, making it possible to observe the videos that showed how children made progress towards learning goals." One teacher assistant described how "...since applying strategies, and making more materials available," dramatic differences in English language arts and math learning developed during circle time. Some educators, however, had concerns about using play-based practices, because the support systems needed to make them work were often lacking. Administrator support was sparse, professional development opportunities were limited, materials were in short supply, and a high-turnover of staff affected the effectiveness of play-based teaching.

Most educators recognized that **choice** fostered children's decision-making in play. Children were motivated through choice, and when given opportunities, readily made decisions about what they wanted to do. Another educator commented how "...offering children choice required me to be flexible and listen to what they said. I had to hold back and allow the child to tell me what she wanted." A third teacher candidate said, "children's own ideas are right there, if you listen to them."

Efficient use of **time** in the daily routine was identified by educators as important. One teacher candidate reported, "Allowing children to have long periods of unbroken time during indoor and outdoor play sessions ensures they have opportunities to think." Making **links** between concepts that children explored during free-play times, small-group times and large-group times, enabled children to have repeated opportunities to explore and understand concepts.

Recording Observations

Participants	Very positive	Positive
Teachers	100%	0%
Teacher Assistants	80%	20%
Teacher Candidates	100%	0%
Team Leaders	40%	60%

Table 8.4: Participants' ratings concerning the recording of observations

Participants' ratings suggested that the recording of observations was a highly effective assessment tool. New teaching skills, employed by teacher assistants specifically observing and assessing children, helped them use strategies to help children make progress. Recording observations ensured that children's learning was monitored and the impact of teaching strategies was seen. Observations of children were commonly recorded under content areas, e.g., math or science. Teacher assistants reported, "Observation made me look more carefully at what children did and made me appreciate their different learning abilities." Another said, "Observation showed how children explored literacy, math and science concepts in play. I see now how I have to reflect that exploration back in my teaching." By closely observing a teacher candidate reported, "I know how to support children's play more effectively, by making enough resources available for them to use." Another said how observation enabled her to better read the classroom and problem-solve during team meetings. She said, "I have evidence and have something definite to say about children's learning."

New teaching strategies led to **changes in assessment roles.** Teacher assistants reported how teachers commonly wrote observations of children. However, some teacher assistants took on new observation roles during small and large-group times that released teachers to focus more on teaching. Teacher assistants worked in partnership with teachers when they shared written observations, assessed children's responses, and planned differentiated activities that responded to children's exact learning needs. Other teacher assistants commented how, "New roles in observation increased professional knowledge about what children learned and what activities were needed to promote their next-steps in learning".

Analysis of observations promoted better **differentiation** of activities. Opportunities existed for each child to respond uniquely by experimenting with materials, and producing different outcomes in play. Teacher candidates explained how during socio-dramatic and in play centers, each child made unique artifacts, that showed their individual thinking. Planning **open-ended** activities enabled differentiation that was supportive of each child's abilities and needs. One teacher candidate commented how satisfying it was to see a child succeed in activities that were planned from observations recorded on video. Children with language delays were asked open-ended questions about how they felt, and responded by pointing to a face on a feelings chart. The addition of more materials supported inclusion as each child's socialization and movement needs were met. This was found to be particularly useful when supporting children with complex behavioral problems.

Video recordings revealed what educators missed in written observations. The entirety of children's learning, including classroom context, children's ideas, language use, and socialization patterns were captured on video. Teachers said, "Children's progress was often under-documented in written observations, and this had serious implications for the accuracy of their reported attainment." Video recordings enabled participants to gain a deeper understanding of children's learning. Teams observed each child both as an individual and also as part of a group. Team viewings were thorough and enabled the planning of activities to support a child's individual needs at designated times in the daily routine. For example, language activities were intentionally planned for circle times, to expand the limited vocabulary of individual children during work-time. Repeated viewings revealed how multiple learning domains and content areas were integrated in play. One teacher explained that math games used in circle time included, "not just the intellectual domain but also social, physical, and language domains."

Videos enabled a complete record of events in classrooms to be assessed, including the impact of strategies. Teachers identified how **checklists** helped in analyzing videos. Analysis was difficult because, "observations happened at the speed of lightning," making it easy to lose track of what to look for. Checklists kept teams focused and ensured that strategies were assessed consistently. They enabled educators to count the number of times particular behaviors occurred, and therefore, evaluate the success of a strategy. Checklists were seen as a positive tool for teams to use because they provided evidence of change resulting from strategy implementation.

Educators reported that there was not enough **time** during team meetings to analyze all observations recorded on video. Teams needed more time to develop a deeper understanding of observations seen on video, and to reflect on events. One educator said, "Finding time to watch the videos was a problem, because it had to be done on a regular basis in order to be able to stay on top of what happened in classrooms."

Applying Content Area Knowledge

Participants	Very positive	Positive
Teachers	20%	80%
Teacher Assistants	0%	100%
Teacher Candidates	20%	80%
Team Leaders	40%	60%

Table 8.5: Participants' ratings concerning the application of content knowledge

Teaching content through **integration** rather than through separate content areas was identified as appropriate for young children because they were not aware of separate content areas in their play. One team leader described how literacy, math, arts and technology were fully integrated in a book making activity.

Using Learning Standards

Participants	Very positive	Positive	Average
Teachers	0%	60%	40%
Teacher Assistants	0%	20%	80%
Teacher Candidates	0%	40%	60%
Team Leaders	0%	60%	40%

Table 8.6: Participants' responses concerning the use of learning standards

Educators reported that the use of learning standards was average. Using standards guided their teaching of content. One teacher said, "I know what content needs to be covered regarding State Standards." A purchased curriculum was used in another setting to ensure state literacy learning standards were met. In another, state kindergarten standards were used to prepare children in Pre-K for the next grade level. Head Start teams used the Head Start Early Learning Framework Outcomes to guide their teaching of separate content areas. Teacher candidates were familiar with NAEYC Standards (2009) and described them as "a great resource to guide their teaching during Practicum." Their understanding of NAEYC Standards (2009) was helped by reading NAEYC journal articles that showed them what NAEYC Standards looked like in practice. One teacher candidate commented, "The journals helped me see how important developmentally-appropriate practice is, and how each lesson should have a definite learning purpose that reflects standards."

Discussion of Teaching Skills

When child development was included in action research, educators targeted their teaching to children's current learning needs. The use of child development literature helped teams fully acknowledge children's typical and atypical developmental characteristics. Children's developmental characteristics influenced what teams did to improve their teaching. Teams checked the appropriateness of teaching strategies alongside the developmental characteristics of children in their classrooms. The developmental appropriateness of teaching strategies was not commonly reported on in journal articles, but consideration of this factor, ensured teams used strategies that were relevant to children's developmental needs. Beneficial opportunities existed in the ELC to use content area knowledge to further develop children's learning (Baldwin, Adams, & Kelly 2009). Child development and content area teaching were both required in Standards. However, to effectively combine both elements in teaching, professional development and teacher education programs need to routinely incorporate these factors, to ensure provision is well-targeted, purposeful and challenging to both children's and teacher candidates' learning (Sakellariou, Rentzou, 2011).

Play-based learning, in which children made choices, was widely supported among educators. However, the necessary inputs enabling children's choices regarding sufficient space, time, and materials in the classroom were often lacking (Mooney, 2000). Until educators and teacher candidates routinely assume the responsibility to organize and equip classroom environments in ways that facilitate children's choices, the quality of children's learning experiences in classrooms will be compromised (Thornton, Crim, & Hawkins, 2009).

Using **developmental domains** as the basis to teach content knowledge was identified as important. When social, physical, linguistic, intellectual, and emotional developmental domains were evident in teaching, educators expressed confidence that children's learning needs were comprehensively met. However, the creative domain was often poorly provided for (Kirkwood, Beavers, 2013). Until the creative domain, that underpins young children's thought and expression, is routinely provided for, the needs of the "whole child" are not met and learning is not balanced.

Observations were critical for educators to have accurate information about each child's learning. Observations helped educators understand their teaching roles and provided for informed discussions during team meetings (Recchia, Beck, 2014). Although educators supported integrated learning approaches, their observations were commonly recorded under content knowledge areas in line with learning standards, rather than child development domains. Observation recorded under content knowledge areas emphasized children's academic learning at the expense of their progress in developmental domains.

Team responses showed broad support for video recordings over written observations (Fadde & Sullivan, 2013). This was because efficient and accurate recordings enabled teams to watch recordings together to evaluate the impact of strategies on teaching challenges, on children's learning, and on educators' practice. Although videos generated accurate recordings of some classroom activity, they did not capture "in the moment" events that were often documented by educators in written observations. Although both written and video-recorded observations were found to be valuable in the documentation of children's progress and the impact of strategies, educators reported they did not have sufficient time to watch and analyze videos (Beck, King, Marshall, 2002).

Some new teaching strategies resulted in more complex teaching roles for educators. These strategies freed teachers to focus on their teaching, while teacher assistants recorded observations of children's learning. New teaching roles showed examples of how educators worked in partnerships. Embracing new teaching roles allowed them to use more advanced teaching skills more directly connected to children's learning than they had done previously (Leggett, Ford, 2013). Using checklists to analyze video recordings enabled educators to focus and interpret what they saw. A better organized approach to assessment resulted in planning differentiated activities that improved the inclusion of children with exceptional needs (Griess, Keat, 2014). Team responses consistently identified that sufficient time was not always available for them to implement new teaching skills. However, time has to be made available if educators are to understand why particular practices are more effective than others in supporting children's and teacher candidates' learning (Lind, 2007).

Most educators thought that **content knowledge** was best taught in an integrated approach because it enabled them to build onto what they observed in children's play. Activity planning did not feature largely in the action research but educators said that "play reflected what children thought about and what interested them." Educators used a variety of approaches to promote concept teaching and learning that included using observations of children's play, standards, commercial programs, themes, and seasonal events (Neuman, 2010). However, educators did not say that they undertook research to strengthen their teaching of content. This suggested that their teaching of concepts and skills may lack depth (Moran, Desrochers, Cavicchi, 2007; Schwartz, S. and Copeland, S. (2010). Commercial programs were cited for stifling the creative planning of activities. Some educators followed scripted manuals to cover literacy content to meet required learning standards (Starnes, 2002). This suggested ambivalence existed between educators who used teaching approaches rooted in child development theory, alongside others who used teaching approaches rooted in Standards (Mooney, 2011.)

Educators' average responses concerning the use of **standards** was explained by them not actually referring to a *specific* set of learning standards they had each used during the ELC. Individual educators implemented one of five *different* sets of learning standards that comprised NAEYC (2009); NAEYC early childhood program standards and criteria; DEC recommended practices; New York State Core Body of Knowledge and Competency area; and Head Start Learning Outcomes. These different sets of learning standards presented a challenge in the ELC because, while educators were familiar with the learning standards used in their own settings, they were not familiar with the different sets of learning standards used in others' settings. As a result, teams could not reflect during team meetings on how far new strategies aligned their practices with NAEYC Standards (2009) used at the college. Instead, alignment of new practices with NAEYC Standards (2009) was carried out at the report-writing stage at the end of the semester. The **absence of standard alignment tables** also prevented teams from reflecting on how far their new teaching practices aligned with NAEYC Standards (2009). Two documents, The Core Body of Knowledge: New York State's Core Competencies for Early Childhood Educators (2012), and The New York State Early Learning Alignment Crosswalk (2012), have since been published that assist in alignment across different sets of learning standards. However, a concern remains on how competency areas provided in these publications are based on perceptions of how practice *should* be, rather than how it really *is*. In addition, no recognition is given to the change process, as revealed in action research, that educators underwent as they grappled with new practices required in Standards, or in response to the complex teaching challenges they faced. The change process provided educators with new professional knowledge and skills gained through practice while working with children. Such authentic professional growth equips educators to contribute to the early childhood field in ways that ensure children's and educators' needs are reflected, both current and dynamic.

There is a critical need for educators and administrators involved in Practicum to regularly participate in cross-agency partnerships so that different sets of learning standards are mutually understood and aligned. Only then can an informed foundation exist to promote consistent practice across agencies (Taylor, Hallam, Charlton, & Wall, 2014).

Inquiry skills

Inquiry skills comprised the use of action research, the reading of literature, data analysis and reflection.

Very positive, positive, and *average* rankings as shown in table 8.4 suggested overall inquiry skills were well developed.

Participants	Very positive	Positive	Average
Teachers	66%	17%	17%
Teacher Assistants	66%	17%	17%
Teacher Candidates	80%	20%	0%
Team Leaders	60%	40%	0%

Table 8.7: Ratings for inquiry skills

Action Research

Inquiry skills embedded in action research were reported to enable educators to better understand their own teaching. The implementation of new teaching strategies helped teachers tackle their teaching problems. Practice-related inquiry "fed right into" teacher assistants' teaching and care of children. Teacher candidates reported that practice-related inquiry was highly supportive of their Practicum experiences because it was "real" and focused on what actually happened in their Practicum classrooms.

Even though action research was practice related, some teachers interpreted strategies in ways that led them to **repeat their current practice**. For example, following the use of a strategy designed to improve children's literacy skills through book making, teachers continued their former practice of writing text for children. This prevented children from developing their "emergent" writing. Some teachers looked for **"new"** strategies to overcome teaching challenges, rather than considering how their existing teaching approaches contributed to challenges. Even when "new" strategies were implemented, some teachers repeated earlier practices that meant teaching challenges did not always improve.

During **team-based** action research, educators' inquiry established common goals to improve their teaching. Power-sharing in action research resulted in greater buy-in that was supportive of coordinated teaching roles and that increased teacher candidates' professionalism. For example, teams depended on teacher candidates to find relevant journal articles, and video classrooms to move the inquiry forward. Team-based inquiry developed teacher candidates' problem-solving skills when they learned to keep focused on teaching challenges, contribute towards discussions, and participate in implementing new teaching practices. Purposeful interaction between teacher candidates, and other team participants, developed focused, professional relationships that promoted continuous learning about teaching over the semester.

Thought-provoking inquiry was fostered through action research as teachers investigated challenges and solutions and what the implications were for children. One teacher reported, "I have a new appreciation of what children bring to the classroom now and how I have to use this in my teaching." Teacher-aides commented, "Seeing the classroom through children's eyes" motivated us to improve play centers and better reflect children's choices and learning needs. Seeing children engage in more physical activity, and more willingly share materials, was encouraging, because play was sustained for longer periods of time. Thought provoking inquiry was developed between educators and teacher candidates when they discussed new applications of child development knowledge, developmentally-appropriate practice, and content area knowledge that "enabled them to include all children despite their varied ability." Teacher candidates described how using their observation and assessment skills resulted in provision that accurately supported children's learning needs. Consideration of the context of teaching challenges enabled teacher candidates to understand that challenges did not exist in isolation, but were directly related to children. For example, some children arrived in their classrooms upset because separation from their parents, after a long car journey, was distressing to them. Other children were unsettled because they spent up to ten hours each day in classrooms to accommodate their parents' work routines. One teacher candidate remarked brightly, "My teaching grew a lot because I now think about children. This was a very good experience for the future." Another said, "My thinking has expanded. I understand more about children's lives now."

Inquiry in action research was facilitated by video recordings that enabled teams to track what happened in classrooms over a semester. Watching videos made teams more "thoughtful about their practice and better able to do their jobs." For example, educators created, modified, and monitored play centers to accommodate the individual language and physical needs of children. As a direct result, some educators discarded inappropriate resources. Others no longer used kindergarten standards in Pre-K classrooms and instead provided what children currently needed.

Inquiry through action research was facilitated through the one-hour weekly team meetings. Educators appreciated how they provided time to study and better understand their work. Regular opportunities existed for teams to think about the action research over the whole semester. Teachers said they were more relaxed and not as rushed. However, the weekly one-hour team-meetings were still not long enough for educators to complete all aspects of the action research.

Insufficient communication with **administrators** about the action research created uncertainty among teachers. Some teachers did not know whether the outcomes of action research would be integrated into current practice. Administrators' irregular participation in the action research was unhelpful because it meant they did not understand the impact of strategies in classrooms. Because of this, effective strategies were not always supported or may not be continued in classrooms after the action research was completed.

Literature

Participants' questionnaire responses showed *very positive* and *positive* rankings for the use of literature in the ELC.

Participants	Very positive	Positive
Teachers	50%	50%
Teacher Assistants	33%	66%
Teacher Candidates	80%	20%
Team Leaders	100%	0%

Table 8.8: Participants' responses concerning the use of literature in the ELC

Literature was identified by educators as a useful resource in promoting inquiry. By reading both reference books and journal articles, educators revised their knowledge of child development and were introduced to new strategies that supported the development of their professional attitudes, stimulated their thinking, and enabled them to review and modify their teaching (Thornton et al. 2009). Readings helped educators develop attitudes open to multiple new strategies, and to recognize that there is often more than one right way to fix teaching challenges. For an entire semester, relevant reading kept educators focused on finding and implementing a strategy to improve their teaching challenge. Team leaders said using literature was efficient because it saved teams from having to invent strategies of their own that may not work. Teacher assistants and teacher candidates said journal articles provided them with knowledge, skills, and strategies that were needed to put teaching challenges right. Journal articles were a constant reference point throughout the action research that helped teams stay on track and generated extensive team-discussion. The ability to choose a strategy was helpful because it promoted joint decision-making. However, one concern was that strategy evaluation was often missed in literature, and made judging how effective strategies might be, before they were implemented, difficult.

The librarian was instrumental in supporting teacher candidates' data-base searches for literature. Locating relevant articles was critical to the success of the action research. However, data-base searches were problematical when some teacher candidates failed to spend enough time identifying precise key words. In some cases, wasted time adversely affected the outcomes of literature searches. Some teachers found access to articles challenging. A lack of Internet access in classrooms at the time and not being members of NAEYC explained the challenges. Obtaining articles was sometimes delayed for some teams and caused them to fall behind in their weekly schedule.

The *suitability* of articles was also sometimes problematical. One teacher went to the library in her own time to find articles that more closely matched her teaching challenge. Journal articles did not always match the full scope of teaching challenges and made it necessary to use more than one article at a time. Other teams preferred to use articles that were published in other journals. This was problematic because it was not known how closely aligned these articles were with NAEYC standards for teacher preparation (2009).

Data recording and analysis

Responses for data recording and data analysis indicated *very positive, positive* and *average rankings*. Overall, rankings suggested these areas featured well in the ELC.

Participants	Very positive	Positive	Average
Teachers	60%	40%	0%
Teacher Assistants	20%	40%	40%
Teacher Candidates	0%	100%	0%
Team Leaders	20%	80%	0%

Table 8.9: Participants' responses to data recording and data analysis in the ELC

Video-recordings provided teams with a complete and accurate method of data **recording** (Knight, Bradley, Hock, Skrtic, Knight, Brasseur-Hock & Hatton, 2012). Teachers were provided with, "insightful vignettes that enabled them to see what they would otherwise have missed." Another commented, "Videos were a valuable tool that enabled me to see child interactions in detail." Teacher candidates reported that each child's response was different, indicating where teaching modifications were required. One teacher candidate said, "Videos showed me how to adapt my teaching to make it more creative." Video recordings enabled team leaders to keep track of what happened between team meetings, and understand the impact of strategies on teams and on children.

Most participants rated data analysis of video recordings as positive. Participants indicated how video analysis revealed more about themselves as educators, than they realized. One said, "I like to step back and understand each child's capabilities, what they each liked to do and what progress each child made over time". Another teacher said, "I want to see what has improved in my teaching up to this point, and what still has to be done." Teacher assistants said that data analysis brought "fresh eyes and multiple perspectives" about how strategies worked because unexpected things happened. For example, how often incidents occurred, what triggered them, how long they lasted, which children were involved, and what educators could do in response. Teacher candidates said that video analysis increased their knowledge of child development. One said, "Videos analysis gave concrete evidence about children's skills so that I do not assume things." Another commented, "I reflect back to when I thought teaching was telling children what to do, but I now know it is about me guiding their ideas so things happen in classrooms." Videos were informative because they revealed what happened in classrooms and helped educators know what questions to ask next in action research.

However, the teacher assistants who ranked data analysis as "average" indicated that "Video cameras were initially distracting to me and to children. They did not give a true picture of classroom activity but in time children ignored them."

Checklists facilitated data analysis of video recordings. Checklists consisted of agreed outcomes from teaching strategies. These lists also helped team members identify what they wanted to look for in videos, and what constituted success in improving teaching challenges. Discussing the same questions on checklists enabled teams to reflect consistently on their action research. Checklists had reassured "overwhelmed" teacher candidates to focus and contribute to discussions. Repeated viewings of videos gave teams several opportunities to check analysis and interpretations. However, insufficient time to carry out all data analysis on videos remained a concern.

Data interpretation provided teams with **new insights** into their action research. They were given more ownership of their practice, while teacher assistants commented on what was revealed about children's learning. Evidence on checklists enabled teacher candidates to understand data interpretation discussions that helped teams interpret data and be open to new insights. For example, educators discussed whether purchased literacy programs were appropriate for children with special needs, and questioned whether teaching approaches used in elementary grades were appropriate for children in Pre-K classrooms.

When educators gained new understanding through action research they showed greater **acceptance** of findings and of the implications for their own classrooms. Educators discussed data collected in their own classrooms because they understood the context of it (Nelson, 2012). Educators were more open to accepting what data showed and discussed what it meant for their own practice. Opportunities for teachers to see themselves on video were generally welcomed (Ruto-Korir & Beer (2012). Changed practices were evident through data interpretation. For example, teachers intentionally used richer language to encourage children's decision-making during play, and used child-development theory to more accurately support children's individual learning needs. New practices showed the impact of teaching in developmentally-appropriate ways. For example, embedding numbers into socio-dramatic play, and during circle times, was shown to be successful. Being involved in planning the "next steps" in activities enabled teacher assistants to actively teach children new relevant concepts and skills (Rossouw, R. (2009).

Dissemination of action research findings was facilitated by working in cross-agency teams. Sharing findings was helped by PowerPoint presentations shown at mini-conferences at the college and at early-childhood state and national conferences. Information sharing about changed teaching practices helped other educators who faced similar teaching challenges in their own classrooms, and indicated the implications for the preparation of teacher candidates in teacher education programs (Branscomb & Etheridge, 2010, Cartmel, McFarlane &Nolan, 2014).

Reflection

Participants' reflections in the ELC were analyzed under the following headings: professional growth; teaching development and collaboration. Responses are reported in order of importance with a discussion section at the end.

Professional Growth

Participants' identified how team reflection in the ELC promoted their **professional** growth. Teachers associated professional growth with a better understanding of events in classrooms. Action research made it easier to reflect because events were "real teaching experiences that were directly connected to what took place with children." Reflection on children's learning in video recordings provided insights. One teacher assistants said,

"It was a surprise to realize that boys were much more capable than we thought. We had it wrong, and boys could do more than we realized." Several teacher candidates commented on the importance of "thinking about teaching before jumping and doing it" and "getting a real handle on all the aspects of teaching so it will work." Team viewing of video recordings helped teacher candidates hear multiple perspectives that developed their own thinking and appreciation of on-going, reflective action research for their professional growth (Nolan, A. 2008). Mini-conferences resulted in better understanding that supported professional growth. When teams met together, they shared their IMovie presentations and where appropriate, replicated strategies in other Practicum settings. Other visits and team presentations spread action research results and supported professional growth among a wider early childhood audience.

Teacher candidates said their philosophy of education was developed through reflection. They built on what they learned in college courses and applied it in classrooms. Reflection helped teacher candidates conceptualize how they wanted to teach children in the future. One said, "I want to be flexible and be open to change." Another expressed, "My own teaching grew a lot through reflection. I learned to think about my teaching in a busy classroom where there are many things to attend to at once."

Educators identified how their professional attitudes towards working collaboratively were changed through reflection. Teachers reported that teaching is never perfect and there is always room for educators to work together to make improvements. One teacher assistant said, "It was a good idea to take and use other people's suggestions so that we don't have to keep reinventing the wheel." Several teacher candidates remarked that they did not have to be frightened to work with others or to try out different things.

A lack of questionnaire responses indicated that teams did not reflect on how well their changed teaching did or did not align with NAEYC Standards (2009) used at the college. This presented an area of concern, and was explained by teams implementing different sets of learning standards that presented a challenge to the action research. While individual team participants were familiar with the learning standards used in their own settings, cross-agency teams were not familiar with the different learning standards used in each-others' settings. As a result, during meetings, teams could not reflect on how far new strategies aligned their practices to NAEYC Standards (2009) used at the college

Teaching Development

Educators reported how reflection supported their teaching development. Observation and assessment were critical areas for the understanding of children's actions and abilities. One teacher candidate said, "observing and interacting with children at the same time was *especially* important to teaching development." Related reflection indicated what "next-step" activities needed to be planned, and provided for children to have repeated opportunities to learn concepts. Reflection on videos enabled educators to make accurate assessments of children's learning that provided information to support teaching development.

Applying child development and learning theory in classrooms encouraged educators to see the classroom through children's eyes, check the impact of strategies on teaching challenges and promote teaching development. Teacher candidates identified how opportunities for children's intellectual development were increased by giving them choices involving decision-making and problem-solving about what they wanted to learn. One reported, "I now realize that my teaching is about seeing that children have opportunities to expand their knowledge and skills."

Teaching development through improved physical provision also featured in teacher candidates' thinking. Improved physical provision was said to promote healthy lifestyles and supported the inclusion of children with behavioral difficulties.

Teaching development resulted from applying early childhood theory and practice in ways that improved classroom challenges. New teaching knowledge and skills enabled educators to be more child-centered. For example, when they improved teaching challenges in their classrooms, they were forced to teach for the present rather than for kindergarten and 1st grade-readiness. Better insights into children's current interests and needs allowed teachers to modify activities more readily. Educators learned about the importance of well-organized classroom layout. For example, when sensory table play was better supported and resourced, children's concentration was sustained. Educators determined that their assumptions about sensory table play were incorrect and accepted the need for their practice to change.

Reflection was supportive of teaching development at different stages of the action research. Regular reflection enabled teams to reflect on the same issue from week to week, and develop their thinking and understanding over time. For example, one team reflected over the semester on the impact (at different stages) of an obstacle course in their classroom, regarding how it met children's developmental and learning needs; how children used it; how educators used it in their teaching; and, finally, whether it overcame the teaching challenge. Another team reflected on the need for well-resourced classrooms with flexible routines that could enable children to move between different play centers in ways that promoted sustained play. Several educators reported how integrated teaching approaches supported children's learning in the circle, book, socio-dramatic, and art centers. Integrated teaching enables children to engage in literacy, math, science, and creative arts activities all at the same time, and thereby experience a richer curriculum.

Teachers commented that reflection was, "both professional and personal." One teacher said, "Reflection is part of you and shows what you believe and how you teach." Regular weekly reflection undertaken by the whole team meant that change was progressive and affected all participants to varying degrees. Changed thinking and changed teaching was recognized as an ongoing process that depended on steps accomplished in the action research cycle. Change was most striking at the end of the semester, when current practice was compared to former practice and beliefs stated at the beginning of the semester. Reflection made it easier for some educators to make changes than for others. Some teachers said the benefits of change were obvious. Other educators were more resistant, because they thought change implied criticism of earlier teaching and care-giving practices.

Most teacher assistants said reflecting promoted their teaching development. From their ruminations on children's learning in video recordings, most educators gained new insights into children's thinking. For example, increasing opportunities for children's own ideas to feature in play had a "marked effect on children's motivation." However, reflecting on new strategies and change was not easy for all educators. Using new approaches to behavior management "was a whole new game" for some educators who had to rethink everything they knew about working with children. Several teacher candidates reported how reflection changed their perceptions of their roles in Practicum classrooms. Change made teacher candidates move from *telling* children what to do and listening to children, and provide support to help them create their own ideas for play. This change fundamentally affected teacher candidates' teaching approaches because as one teacher candidate said, "Children's own ideas for play were so much better than mine... because they included so many imaginative ideas for learning." Other teacher candidates reported how team reflection was an efficient way to support teaching development. Several remarked how it would have taken much longer for them to realize that "children learned on the move, in well-resourced classrooms, with responsive educators, where they made choices and decisions about what they wanted to do."

Collaboration

Collaboration was critical to reflection because educators were provided with opportunities to learn from each other about classroom challenges and options for improvement. Educators enjoyed the social nature of collaboration because teaching ideas were exchanged that resulted in team members helping each other in classrooms. One teacher candidate remarked, "Reflection helped me expand my own ideas, but at the same time learn from others."

In teams, educators were motivated to reflect on issues directly relevant to their own teaching. Teacher assistants reported how useful reflective collaboration was and meant that "time spent *supporting* children in learning activities increased and time spent *disciplining* children decreased." Reflective collaboration promoted changed understanding among educators about how children learned. Teacher assistants reported how discussions enabled them to appreciate that children learned "on the move and not when they were made to stay still."

Team leaders commented on the importance of reflective collaboration among cross-agency teams. Discussions reflected varied perspectives that enabled reflection on broad early childhood curriculum issues, e.g., what effect do scripted literacy programs have on the literacy development of children living in poverty; and what is the value of circle time unless it is differentiated to meet children's individual needs? Discussions enabled teacher candidates to build on information they learned in college courses and reflect how it appeared in classrooms. For example, recording observations provided valuable insights into children's learning, but recording observations and interacting with children at the same time was demanding.

Discussion of Action Research as an Inquiry Skill

Broad support for practice-based action research existed among educators because it developed a deeper understanding of their own teaching in their own classrooms (Bleach, 2013). If educators, including teacher candidates, learn effectively about their teaching through action research in classrooms, then emphasis on practice-based action research is recommended in teacher education and professional development programs (Souto-Manning, Mitchell, 2010). This calls for college faculty members, community leaders, administrators, and educators in Practicum classrooms, to work in partnership to they must ensure that contextual information about settings is shared and enables practice-based action research to consistently feature in candidates' professional development. So the early childhood workforce as a whole learns about the act of teaching through their own actions in their own classrooms.

Video cameras, enabled teams to inquire into their classrooms, changed educators' roles from teaching *in* them to also studying the classrooms themselves. Teaching without associated study, threatens the development of better practices in classrooms. Inquiry made educators function through professional knowledge. It also forged a link between professional knowledge and professional practice that served to give most educators a better understanding of their actions in classrooms. However, some educators resisted making changes to their teaching. Change is acknowledged to be a complex and demanding process that requires energy, commitment, time, and support to bring about. The concepts of professional change for professional growth are recommended to feature more strongly in both teacher education and professional development programs so that educators understand that their learning is never "done" but is ongoing and integral to the role of teacher (Moran, 2007).

The importance of teamwork was repeated throughout the action research and showed that improved teaching was not brought about by individuals working on their own, but required educators to collaborate to be effective and consistent (Waite & Davis, (2006).

Insufficient time was made available for educators to carry out all aspects of action research over the semester. Practical problems existed because many Practicum classrooms already function for up to ten hours each day, leaving educators little or no time to meet in teams. Inconsistent participation by administrators in action research was criticized by educators. A review of how they spend their time was requested. Commitment from administrators to attend professional development team meetings and participate in professional learning themselves would support growth among educators.

Discussion of Literature as an Inquiry Skill

The literature places comparatively little emphasis on the critical role of teams using published research to improve teaching challenges in their classrooms. Less emphasis still is made of the contribution that educators make when they transform themselves during action research into data gatherers, evaluators, and reporters of the impact of implementing teaching strategies in their classrooms. Transformational roles enabled educators to not only use literature during team meetings, but also contribute to action research through the practical implementation of strategies focused on teaching improvement in their classrooms (Mesquita-Pires, 2012).

However, some teacher candidates did not fulfill all aspects of their team responsibilities in the action research on time. This problem calls for teacher education faculty to address such concerns and examine how they prepare teacher candidates to work in teams during Practicum (Lattimer, 2012). A lack of internet access in classrooms prevented teams from carrying out online searches, and agencies unaffiliated with NAEYC, prevented some teams from accessing NAEYC journals online. Other teams *wanted* to use non-NAEYC journals, but articles in other journals may not have been aligned, or have been known to be aligned with NAEYC standards for the preparation of teachers (2009). These problems illustrated how fragmentation in settings impeded the implementation of the action research. Calls for collaboration among early childhood agencies at agency and community levels are needed to provide favorable conditions concerning the following: teacher candidates' readiness to work in teams; internet access in classrooms; membership to professional organizations; and standards alignment among agencies in support of professional development.

Discussion of Data Recording and Analysis as Inquiry Skills

Checklists provided consistent ways for teams to analyze video recording data. Consistency allowed for reliable findings. The use of the same questions in checklists enabled consistent weekly discussion in team meetings that, in turn, focused team reflection. Checklists gave educators control over data analysis methods that strengthened their commitment to findings. However, 40% of teacher assistants ranked data analysis as only "average" because they questioned the authenticity of video camera recordings. This finding repeated the need for action research to be carried out within long-established professional relationships, and in safe-guarded environments that ensure both children's and educators' participation is accurately portrayed and used ethically. Several educators reported they were self-conscious about appearing in video recordings. Such a finding shows and must only ever be used to help and never cause educators anxiety (Robson, 2011).

Data analysis facilitated by checklists, and interpretation of videos, supported teams developing new insights into the impact of teaching strategies. Checklists helped teams stay focused during data analysis. These checklists helped teacher candidates, who, as the least experienced participants, used them to support their understanding of data analysis findings. Data interpretation enabled teams to reflect on their teaching and formulate their own evaluations. The presence of administrators at this point in the action research was shown to be pivotal to the adoption of changed practices. Action research findings increased teams' autonomy over their professional development. Collaborative data analysis increased democracy in classrooms (Bleach, 2014).

Team leaders developed leadership skills that maintained teams' focus, and that created a link between evaluation and reflection. Team leaders were instrumental in supporting the unique professional development needs of each team. If team leaders are pivotal to the success of professional development teams, their leadership skills need to be clearly identified, conceptualized, and used to lead professional development programs. PowerPoint presentations portrayed educators in a new role as agents of change in their own classrooms. The first steps to bring educators from different agencies to work together were taken. However, more frequent interaction between different agencies was needed to build relationships that could share information for change and improvement in classrooms. A dilemma existed for teams involving video recordings that created permanent data sources about classrooms, but ironically the teams did not have sufficient time to fully analyze them.

Discussion of Reflection as an Inquiry Skill

When educators reported that professional growth developed through reflection, it was also shown to be rooted in classroom experiences. The action research model of professional growth contrasted with more common models of professional development that were unrelated to the context of classrooms and detached from educators' own teaching experiences with children. This suggests that early childhood professional development models are most effective when they include elements educators report as crucial to their professional growth.

Reflection provided educators with deeper insights into children's learning and their own related practice. On occasion, educators recognized that aspects of their current practice were in error (Jensen, B. Holm, A & Bremberg, S. 2013).

Reflection revealed how educators critically examined and evaluated their own practice, and worked to improve it. Therefore, when given optimum time and conditions to reflect, most educators could effectively monitor their own practice and make changes to bring about improvements. Teacher candidates showed how reflection on journal articles let them define teaching challenges more clearly, reconstructing their thinking about teaching practices. This suggests that to better prepare candidates to cope with challenges in theoretical classrooms, thinking-based, problem-solving activities based in *real* classrooms, should be utilized.

Team meetings gave educators regular opportunities to reflect on teaching challenges. Educators assimilated what each said to further inform their thoughts in support of their professional growth. The reported merits of team meetings, mini-conferences, and visits between settings, were striking because they fostered collaboration... with the objective of securing improved teaching in classrooms. In doing so, a professional development model existed, built on collaboration, to improve teaching knowledge and skills among participants at different stages in their professional development.

This model acted as an alternative to the more traditional external and authoritarian models that impose practices, often unrelated to the context of their classrooms, or the needs of the children in them. Educators reported how regularly scheduled reflection enabled them to examine complex aspects of their practice that may have been too demanding for educators to do on their own. With these meetings, educators were in a better position to connect observation, assessment, planning and reflection in teaching. Teams garnered a deeper understanding of how aspects of practice were best used together to create smooth teaching operations that benefitted everyone.

Educators' knowledge of child development and learning theory was important for interpreting their findings. Firmly locating professional development models—within child development knowledge—ensured that early childhood teaching was child-centered and the impact on children was beneficial. This made educators teach to children's *current* learning needs, as indicated by assessment and teaching challenges, rather than in preparation for the next grade level.

Team reflection touted the importance of well-organized and adequately resourced classrooms. Less apparent was educators' response to classrooms that lacked those qualities. Educators are the architects of classrooms, and it is their responsibility to gather appropriate free materials, in adequate supplies, to ensure that children have what they need to develop their learning in play. Educators could, for example, ask families to provide regular clean supplies, gather seasonal natural materials, and ask local businesses to donate surplus items

Weekly reflection over a semester revealed how educators' thinking developed at different times and in different ways. The pivotal role of team leaders in asking focused questions, was to reveal the thinking that hindered action research progress. The different starting points among educators, and the different rate at which they were able to comprehend issues, were highlighted. Team leaders' leadership skills were instrumental in team progress and needed to be harnessed for use in professional development programs.

Reflection clearly affected educators' personal and professional development. Some showed their adaptability by comparing their earlier and later thinking about the teaching challenges they faced, and revealed their attitudes toward change. By acknowledging *former* thinking, opportunities were created to express new insights that demonstrated their enlightenment about optimum conditions for both children's learning and for their teaching. Change was more difficult for some educators than for others. This suggested that professional development is most effective when carried out over an extended period, within a supportive professional relationship, to bolster professional growth.

Reflection was easier to achieve by working in teams. Social and collaborative teamwork enabled educators to discuss their action research together, and to help each other with their teaching. The explosion of online forums will serve to facilitate this in the future.

Educators' responses suggest it is right to require educators to use social and collaborative approaches to teaching, because of the useful impact they have on wise decision-making in early childhood classrooms. The implications for teacher preparation programs suggest that teacher candidates be prepared, not as teachers who independently carry out their own practices and assignments, but as educators who work collaboratively to carry out assignments with input and support from others. Teams in the ELC were comprised of educators who worked in different agencies. However, historical factors explain the different practices, curricula and learning standards in different agencies involved in Practicum. These factors are overshadowed by the unifying truth that there is only one early childhood field in which teaching challenges are to be dealt with, in ways that benefit for the whole early childhood field, and for all individuals involved in it. The need for more collaboration between agencies, so that coordinated responses are effectively developed towards consistent professional actions, is clear.

Conclusion

The ELC revealed how the context of children's play was a critical force in growing educators' professional development. Play consisted of everything that was known to be important and meaningful to children and included their families, friends, actions, materials, languages, ideas, creativity and feelings as well as routines and materials made available to them.

The ELC demonstrated how educators' professional development occurred through the deliberate and purposeful implementation of strategies as they involved themselves in children's play. When developmentally appropriate strategies were planted in play, educators created and improved opportunities for children to explore concepts, content, skills and dispositions in ways that were relevant, interesting and challenging to children. The implementation of strategies enabled educators to change into observers of play, implementers of strategies and assessors of children's responses as they worked to overcome challenges in their classrooms.

The primary interest of the authors was to develop professional development opportunities to improve and increase the knowledge and teaching skills of teacher candidates and of educators during Practicum. The table below indicates how this was accomplished throughout the course of the ELC and how, in particular, play was instrumental in all facets of teaching and learning, to secure improved practice.

Factors	Impact	Positive	Negative	Implications
ELC design	Created professional development model aimed at improving teaching challenges and improving consistency between teaching in college and practice during Practicum field experience.	Enabled professional development teams consisting of participants from college, the community and Practicum settings to be formed. Allowed improved practice to develop and spread across settings to build greater consistency of practice.	It was not understood in the grant design that different sets of learning standards were used at the college and different and varied learning standards were used in Practicum settings. Team participants' unfamiliarity with the different sets of standards and a lack of published alignment tables made alignment between college teaching and Practicum practice impossible to achieve during the semester.	To promote consistent practice in Practicum settings, it is necessary that learning standards and standards alignment tables are published and distributed concurrently to colleges and to Practicum settings.
Educators' professional development	Teams' professional development occurred through studying teaching challenges based in their own classrooms	In all case studies, when new teaching strategies were embedded into the context of children's play, the strategies were effective in improving both the teaching challenges and educators' practices.	Some educators resisted using new strategies and resisted changed practice because it undermined their control in the classroom.	Emphasize in literature and in standards documents that children's play is a most effective vehicle to bring about educators' improved teaching. Professional development is best undertaken over time because time is needed for some educators to change their practice.

Factors	Impact	Positive	Negative	Implications
Literature	Teams carried out data-base searches to find developmentally appropriate literature related to the teaching challenges they faced in their classrooms.	Candidates became readers of literature that built their professional knowledge and skills.	It was not always possible to find just one research article that addressed one teaching problem. It was sometimes necessary to use more than one journal article. A lack of Internet access in classrooms hindered the accessing of literature.	Register teams for NAEYC Membership. Organize Internet access in classrooms to ensure professional literature can be accessed whenever needed.
Technology	Technology enabled teams to investigate and record data about their teaching challenges.	Video-recording enabled teams to see and understand teaching challenges and collaborate for improvement. Audio tapes enabled team meeting discussions to be recorded, downloaded and stored for analysis. IMovie presentations enabled teams to share their teaching improvements at local and state conferences.	One-hour weekly team meetings did not provide enough time for team viewing and analysis of all videos and audio tapes	Equip each Practicum classroom with the technology and electronic devices they need. Allow more time during team meetings to analyze collected data so findings are evident and understood by the team.
Action Research	Teams followed a prescribed professional development format.	Teams turned into problem-solvers, data gatherers and decision makers connected directly to their own classroom practice. Inbuilt discussion and reflection time ensured professional growth.	Some educators resisted change.	Recommended that professional development time has to be specified in educators' contracts of employment.

Finally, the ELC revealed that play, when appropriately supported by educators, is not only the critical medium for all children's learning and development, but is, at the same time, the critical medium for educators' associated professional development. It is therefore incumbent on policy makers to unequivocally emphasize the importance of the medium of play in early childhood policy, standards and curriculum documentation.

9. CONCLUSION

Evidence from the case studies included in this book, participants' questionnaire responses and feedback from team leaders and the college librarian are used to evaluate the ELC professional development model and make recommendations for further improvement. The evaluation is carried out to assess how well the stated aims of the ELC were met and written under strengths and weaknesses headings. Recommendations are made to further improve the ELC model. To recap, the aims of the ELC were to: (1) build professional development connections between early childhood educators in different agencies involved with Practicum; (2) align educators' practice in Practicum placements with NAEYC Standards (2009) used at the College; and, (3) demonstrate the impact of the ELC on the learning of team participants and on children in Practicum placements.

The Evaluation of the ELC

(1) Build professional development connections between early childhood educators in different agencies involved with Practicum.

Evidence suggests that overall this aim was met but recommendations were made to overcome weaknesses. On the strengths side, the design of the ELC was critical in building professional development connections between early childhood educators in different agencies involved with Practicum. Early childhood faculty at the College acted as a catalyst to reach out to long-standing and trusted early childhood partners who already participated in the Practicum field experience. These partners included directors and educators in preschool agencies, professionals in the Childcare Council, plus a new connection with the librarian in the Teaching Materials Center, TMC, in the College Library. These inter-agency partners created professional connections between diverse groups that resulted in the scope of the ELC being more far reaching, and the impact of Action Research, spread consistent practice more widely among team members and the agencies in which they were each based.

The creation of inter-agency professional development teams in Practicum placements ensured the ELC operated in classrooms and focused on professional development that used an Action Research approach to investigate teaching challenges identified by educators in their classrooms. Central to the investigation was to improve the quality of educators' and teacher candidates' teaching, and as a direct consequence, improve the quality of learning opportunities made available to children.

Secure grant funding was one crucial factor in making the ELC function effectively. It paid for team leaders from the Childcare Council to guide teams through their Action Research. It paid preschool agencies to provide coverage to free educators in Practicum classrooms from their normal teaching duties. Those educators were then able to attend weekly, hour-long team meetings, to work collaboratively with their team leader and teacher candidate on their Action Research. Grant funding also paid for the purchase of technology that was essential to the work of the ELC, used by designated team members to accurately record data and monitor the impact of Action Research over the semester.

On the weaknesses side, the ELC design omitted to include a requirement for preschool directors to regularly participate, although some did voluntarily. It was mistakenly thought that Action Research was targeted only at improving educators' and teacher candidates' practice in Practicum classrooms. However, it was apparent that without directors' knowledge and support for team Action Research, change to improve either the curriculum or teaching methods, was unlikely to be understood, supported or be sustained. Hour-long team meetings were found to be too short for teams to cover all aspects of their Action Research.

Recommendations for future improvements are:

- Require directors of preschool agencies who host teacher candidates during Practicum to routinely participate in Action Research. Directors are then more likely to understand the team rationale for new teaching approaches and support change in classrooms.
- Increase cover in classrooms to allow educators to be released from their teaching for longer time each week. When teams meet for longer at weekly team meetings, they are more likely to complete their Action Research in a timely manner.

(2) Improve and align educators' practice in Practicum placements with NAEYC Standards (2009) used at the College;

Evidence suggests that this aim was partly met. Recommendations are made to address weaknesses. On the strengths side, ample evidence indicated that Action Research was instrumental in teams developing a wide range of analytical skills, that were highly supportive of their improved professional understanding and their related practice in their classrooms. These analytical skills were honed as teams developed a problem-solving stance to the teaching challenges they faced.

The video recordings of team members at work in their own classrooms, with their own children, enabled them to observe teaching challenges and assess what might cause them. For example, only when watching a video, did one teacher candidate notice the sensory table in the classroom and how rarely children used it. Throughout the semester, teams watched videos that showed the impact of strategies and gained new insights about their teaching. For example, preparing more active and differentiated literacy games to use during Circle time, provided educators with valuable information about what affected children's levels of engagement during activities.

The provision of sufficient guided discussion and reflection time during team meetings was critical for teams' improved understanding of their teaching. This pertained to the topics of the case studies, which included: diversity and ESL learners; gender and challenging behavior; uncovering hidden beliefs about children's mathematical understanding and observing what children represented in play. Additional topics discussed during team meetings included children's science content and evaluating classroom space.

Reflection on videos resulted in new understanding and changed roles in classrooms. Teacher assistants described changing their work from "policing" children to writing observations. This enabled teachers to plan and teach developmentally appropriate "next step" learning activities.

Teams' reading of professional literature was a critical strength in promoting improved practice in Practicum placements. The librarian's role in supporting teacher candidates' searches to find relevant literature developed their ability to better understand and more precisely define teaching challenges to select beneficial journal articles for their team to read. Journal articles provided teams with proven strategies were known to work and improved teaching. Regular professional reading among teams encouraged team members to increase their teaching knowledge and skills and be current with research findings. Reading reputable child development peer reviewed journals was particularly effective in enabling teams to weave DAP into their Action Research and to understand and apply child development theory in their practice. Teacher candidates commented how reading literature helped them write better lesson plans that were DAP and reflected NAEYC standards. One teacher candidate commented how reading literature gave her firm ideas about what and how to teach children so that it was no longer guess-work.

On the weaknesses side, it was evident that to improve **and** align educators' practice in Practicum placements with NAEYC Standards (2009), were two separate processes and not one. Although Action Research provided compelling evidence of improved practice, alignment of that practice with NAEYC standards was not. This was because initial ELC training focused only on NAEYC standards (2009) which were used at the college and were familiar to faculty members and teacher candidates. It was not understood that community professionals (who worked as team leaders), preschool directors and educators in Practicum placements were not familiar with NAEYC standards (2009). More surprising was that preschool agencies that hosted Practicum placements, each used one of five different sets of early childhood learning standards. The use of these other sets of standards may explain why educators were not familiar with NAEYC standards (2009) and, why teacher candidates sometimes had difficulty in completing their required assignments during Practicum. It also explained why teams were unable to align their changed practice with NAEYC Standards (2009) or were not able to fully reflect on alignment during team meetings, and why evaluation of alignment was delayed until the write-up stage of case studies.

Concerning teams' reading literature, it was not always possible for teacher candidates to find just one journal article that provided strategies to overcome all aspects of their teaching challenges. Preschool agencies commonly were not members of NAEYC and this prevented teams from accessing NAEYC data bases themselves if needed. Teams' lack of Internet access in classrooms also compounded this problem.

Some educators resisted change through Action Research in their classrooms because changed practice was believed to confuse children and undermine those educators' control of teaching situations and of children's behavior.

A lack of readiness in some teacher candidates affected how they worked in teams and carried out required tasks. Throughout the semester an important task was to complete a PowerPoint presentation of the action research at the end of the semester; the task was not completed.

Recommendations to facilitate the successful improvement and alignment of educators' practice in Practicum placements with NAEYC Standards (2009) is:

- During initial ELC training, use a common language to familiarize all ELC participants with both NAEYC standards (2009) and with the different sets of standards used in each preschool agency.
- During initial training, use a common language to familiarize teams with standard alignment tables that enable them to evaluate how far their changed practice aligns with NAEYC standards (2009) and with the standards used in their own settings.
- Prepare teacher candidates, if necessary, to find several journal articles that provide multiple strategies to address all aspects of their one teaching challenge.
- Encourage preschool agencies to become members of NAEYC or another professional membership that will enable them to routinely access NAEYC or other professional journals.
- In the preschool building, provide teams with Internet access to support their Action Research.
- In ELC initial training, familiarize team members with change theory to help educators understand that change is often unsettling and takes time to adjust to.

- At the college prepare teacher candidates to work in teams during Practicum.

(3) demonstrate the impact of the ELC on the professional learning of team participants and on children in Practicum placements.

Evidence suggests this aim was met. The impact of the ELC in promoting the professional learning of team participants, including children, was evident. Planting agreed strategies in play was key to educators' and teacher candidates' improved professional learning and improved teaching during Practicum.

In the ELC, children's play was recognized as the critical vehicle in growing educators' professional development and occurred as educators proactively and purposefully applied strategies by embedding them into children's play. Play incorporated everything that was important and meaningful to children and was widely accepted to effectively promote children's learning and development in all areas that related to their families and friends, actions, intentions, use of materials, acquisition of language, representation of ideas, expression of creativity and demonstration of feelings.

Each case study in this book illustrates how teams implemented strategies, for example, the "talking time" strategy to create opportunities for children to express their own ideas for socio-dramatic play. A science area created opportunities for children to explore materials and construct scientific concepts through free-play. A physical play area in the classroom gave children new opportunities to move and explore space. A sensory table allowed children to choose and use varied materials to make up stories and play out scenarios. A guidance process and a feelings chart supported children to express their emotions appropriately in play. Games and active learning activities introduce play into Circle time.

Educators took on the role of architects of rich play as they proactively implemented deliberate, developmentally-appropriate, purposeful strategies into children's play. This deliberate act created critical opportunities for children to explore concepts, understand content, develop new skills and exhibit learning dispositions that are relevant, interesting and challenging to children. In response to children's demonstrated play, it was evident how educators had to use their professional analytical skills, developed through Action Research to sustain the play and children's learning within it. This involved observing, talking, interacting as appropriate in the play and assessing children at play so educators have information to further develop it.

The ELC shows us that for educators to continue to improve their professional skills during professional development, it is incumbent on policy makers to unequivocally state in early childhood policy, learning standards and curriculum documentation, that play is the vehicle through which all children's learning develops, and at the same time, best facilitates educators' associated professional development.

APPENDIX A: EDUCATORS' QUESTIONNAIRE

Educators' questionnaire

Pre and Post Action Research

Interview to be carried out and recorded by team leader

1. Rate your feelings towards your Early Childhood work at this time (check one rating)

    (a) very positive(b) positive(c) average(d) negative(e) very negative

    Explain your rating

2. Rate your ability to effectively use Early Childhood child development knowledge in your classroom at this time (check one rating)

    (a) very high(b) high(c) average(d) low(e) very low

    Explain your rating

3. Rate your ability to effectively use content knowledge in your classroom at this time (check one rating)

    (a) very high(b) high(c) average(d) low(e) very low

Explain your rating

4. What kinds of professional development have you had in the past? (check as many from this list as you wish):

   • workshops

- college courses
- speakers
- CDA
- conferences
- video
- poster presentations
- visiting other settings
- mentoring
- other (please specify)

5. What kinds of professional development have you found to be most useful? (check as many types from this list as you wish):

- workshops(f) college courses
- speakers(g) CDA
- conferences(h) video
- poster presentations(i) visiting other settings
- mentoring(j) other (please specify)

Please explain your checks

6. What is your attitude towards this Action Research professional development right now? (please check one)

(a) very positive(b) positive(c) average (d) negative(e) very negative

Explain your rating

7. Rate how do you feel about working in an Action Research team right now. (Please check one)

(a) very positive(b) positive(c) average (d) negative(e) very negative

Explain your rating

8. Rate how you feel about a SUNY Practicum student being in your team. (Please check one)

(a) very positive(b) positive(c) average (d) negative(e) very negative

Explain your rating

8. How do you feel about using NAEYC publications to guide your Action Research. (Please check one)

(a) very positive(b) positive(c) average (d) negative(e) very negative

Explain your rating

9. How do you feel about using a video recorder in your classroom as part of the Action Research. (Please check one)

(a) very positive(b) positive(c) average (d) negative(e) very negative

Explain your rating

10. How do you feel about analyzing the video recordings as part of the Action Research. (Please check one)

(a) very positive(b) positive(c) average (d) negative(e) very negative

Explain your rating

11. How do you feel about interpreting the video recordings as part of the Action Research. (Please check one)

(a) very positive(b) positive(c) average (d) negative(e) very negative

Explain your rating

12. What do you feel about creating a documentation panel to share your Action Research with other teams (Please check one)

(a) very positive(b) positive(c) average (d) negative(e) very negative

Explain your rating

13. What do you hope to get out of this Action Research professional development?

14. What do you hope your setting will get out of this Action Research professional development?

APPENDIX B: TEACHER CANDIDATES' QUESTIONNAIRE

Teacher Candidates' Questionnaire

To be completed at the end of the semester

1. How did this research project enable you to professionally interact with Early Childhood educators?
2. How did this research project affect your relationship with children?
3. Did the project change your attitude toward teaching young children?
4. How did the research foster your inquiry into teaching young children?
5. What have you learned in this research project that will affect your Early Childhood teaching in any of these areas: (a) classroom management; curriculum development; inclusion; differentiation; family involvement; assessment?
6. How did the research project foster your problem-solving skills to improve your own teaching?
7. How did the research project foster your reflection on your own teaching?
8. What teaching challenges are you now aware of that the Early Childhood program needs to prepare you for?

LIST OF TABLES

PART 1

CHAPTER 1

PART II

CHAPTER 2

CHAPTER 3

CHAPTER 4

LIST OF FIGURES

GLOSSARY OF ELC TERMS

Action Research: A form of self-reflective enquiry undertaken by early childhood participants designed to improve their teaching and their understanding of it.

Administrator: An individual responsible for the implementation of regulations, policies and operations in an early childhood agency.

Agency: A provider of preschool educational and care services to young children and their families.

National Association for Child Care Resource and Referral Agency (NACCRA): Referred to as the Area Child Care Council (ACCC) that promotes national policies and partnerships to advance the development and learning of all children, and to promote vision, leadership and support to community child care, resource and referral agencies.

Care: Meaning that the holistic needs and wellbeing of every individual in the preschool are met with kindness and respect.

Case study: A detailed examination of one Practicum classroom. Examination of multiple classrooms would constitute a *collective* case study.

Categories: Data is organized into patterns and themes during qualitative analysis.

Child Development Associate: The CDA qualification is earned through an agency with expert early childhood teacher preparation knowledge. It involves 120 hours of early childhood education covering the growth and development of children aged 3 to 5 years.

College: A higher education institution in which early childhood practicum students, are prepared to teach children from birth through age 8.

Conference: A meeting where early childhood teams present and share their Action Research work with other early childhood practitioners.

Constructivism: A theory put forward by Piaget that children build their own learning through actions on their environment.

Cross-agency: Collaboration across different early childhood institutions and agencies designed to promote consistent high quality early childhood educational and care practices.

Developmentally Appropriate Practice (DAP): As defined by NAEYC: a framework of principles and guidelines for best practice in the care and education of young children, birth through age 8. It is grounded in the research on how young children develop and learn and in what is known about education effectiveness. The principles and guidelines outline practice that promotes young children's optimal learning and development. (Citation)

Director: An individual who is in charge of a preschool.

Field experiences: The time that early childhood teacher candidates spend in early childhood classrooms that is a requirement for their early childhood degree.

iMovie: A video editing software program that enables Macintosh computer users to edit their own movies. by importing video footage.

Learning community: A group of early childhood staff from different agencies that undertook a semester of professional development together during Practicum.

Literature: Published articles in early childhood professional journals.

NAEYC: The National Association for the Education of Young Children is a leading organization in USA regarding the care, learning and development of young children birth through 8 years.

NCATE: The National Council for the Accreditation of Teacher Education works to establish high quality teacher preparation through the process of professional accreditation of colleges.

OCFS: The Office of Children and Family Services serves the public by promoting the safety, permanency and wellbeing of children, families and communities.

PowerPoint: A computer software program that enables Practicum students to construct slides and create presentations.

Practicum: The first extensive 75-hour field experience in the early childhood teacher education program.

Practicum candidates: Practicum candidates work during Practicum field hours with an experienced early childhood teacher as they interact with children and teachers during classroom activities, routines and complete required assignments.

Preschool: Preschools provide care and education for children aged 3 – 5 years and focus on their social, physical, language, intellectual and creative development. Preschools may be owned and operated as private or parochial schools.

Pre-Kindergarten: Pre-K Can be located in public schools, private schools or daycare centers. It focuses on the care and education the whole child in close partnership with families.

Professional development: Opportunities offered to teacher candidates and early childhood teachers during Practicum that was designed to improve teaching challenges faced in classrooms.

Qualitative data analysis: Involves three stages: (1) Data reduction when collated and summarized in categories; (2) Data display when displayed in charts or diagrams; (3) Conclusions drawn when results are described in words.

Quantitative data analysis: The use of numbers to make sense of data.

Reflection: Teachers' careful consideration of classroom video recordings for improved future teaching.

Setting: A preschool with classrooms for children aged 3-5 years in which a Practicum student is placed.

Teachers: All adults working in a setting who assume the role of teacher or assistant teacher-teacher aide.

Teaching: Comprising all routines, practices and activities in Practicum classrooms concerned with the education and care of young children aged 3-5 years.

Teaching Materials Center (TMC): A college-based teaching and learning resource center for teacher candidates and for the community at large to use.

REFERENCES

Albrecht, K.M. & Engel, B. (2007). Moving away from a quick mentality to systematic professional development. *Young Children*, 62(4).

Arhar, J.M., Holly, M.L., & Kasten, W.C. (2001). *Action Research for Teachers Traveling the Yellow Brick Road*. New Jersey: Merrill Prentice Hall.

Bainer, D.L., & Wright, D. (2000). Teachers' choices about their own professional development in science teaching and learning. In D.J. McIntyre & D.M. Byrd (Eds.) *Research on effective models for teacher education* (pp. 44-61). Thousand Oaks, Calif: Corwin; London: Sage.

Baker, F. (2014). A pathway to play in early childhood education developed through the explicit modelling of reflective practice in teacher education in Abu Dhabi, UAE. *Reflective Practice*, 15(2), 203-217. doi:10.1080/14623943.2014.883306

Baldwin, J. L., Adams, S. M., & Kelly, M. (2009). Science at the center: An emergent, standards-based, child-centered framework for early learners. *Early Childhood Education Journal*, 37(1), 71-77. doi:10.1007/s10643-009-0318-z

Beck, R. J., King, A., & Marshall, S. K. (2002). Effects of video case construction on preservice teachers' observations of teaching. *Journal of Experimental Education*, 70(4), 345-361. doi:10.1080/00220970209599512

Bekleyen, N. (2011). Can I teach English to children? Turkish pre-service teacher candidates and very young learners. *Journal of Early Childhood Teacher Education*, 32(3), 256-265. doi:10.1080/10901027.2011.594700

Bishop, K. K. (1993). Interagency collaboration and transition. In *Family/professional collaboration for children with special needs and their families*. Retrieved from http://pacer.org/tatra/resources/inter.asp

Bleach, J. (2013). Using action research to support quality early years' practice. *European Early Childhood Education Research Journal*, 21(3), 370-379. doi:10.1080/1350293X.2013.814354

Bleach, J. (2014). Developing professionalism through reflective practice and ongoing professional development. *European Early Childhood Education Research Journal*, 22(2), 185-197. doi:10.1080/1350293X.2014.883719

Branscomb, K., & Ethridge, E. A. (2010). Promoting professionalism in infant care: Lessons from a yearlong teacher preparation project. *Journal of Early Childhood Teacher Education*, 31(3), 207-221. doi:10.1080/10901027.2010.500513

Brown, M. S., Bergen, D., & House, M. (2000). An observational study: Examining the relevance of developmentally appropriate practices, classroom adaptations, and parental participation in the context of an integrated preschool program. *Early Childhood Education Journal*, 28(1), 51-56

Bruno, H. E. (2007) Gossip-free zones: Problem-solving to prevent power struggles. *Young Children*, 62(5). 26-33.

Butler, D.L. & Schnellert, L. (2012). Collaborative inquiry in teacher professional development. *Teaching and Teacher Education, 28,* 1206-1220.

Cartmel, J., Macfarlane, K., & Nolan, A. (2013). Looking to the future: producing transdisciplinary professionals for leadership in early childhood settings. *Early Years: Journal of International Research & Development, 33*(4), 398-412. doi:10.1080/09575146.2013.852522

Cartwright, T. (2012). Science talk: Preservice teachers facilitating science learning in diverse afterschool environments. *School Science & Mathematics,* 112(6), 384-391. doi:10.1111/j.1949-8594.2012. 00147.x

Chen, J. & Horsch, P. (2004). *Effective partnering for school change.* Teachers College Press. New York.

Christ, T., & Wang, X. C. (2013). Exploring a community of practice model for professional development to address challenges to classroom practices in early childhood. *Journal of Early Childhood Teacher Education, 34* (4), 350-373.

Clark, P., & Huber, L. (2005). Enhancing early childhood teacher growth and development through professional development school partnerships. *Journal of Early Childhood Teacher Education, 26*(2), 179-186. doi:10.1080/10901020590955743

Cochran-Smith, M., & Lytle, S. L. (1993). *Inside/Outside: Teacher research and knowledge.* Teachers College Press: New York.

Core body of knowledge: New York State's core competencies for early childhood educators. Retrieved from: http://www.earlychildhood.org/pdfs/CoreBody.pdf

Darling-Hammond, L. (2000). How teacher education matters. *Journal of Teacher Education,* 51(3), 166-173.

Dick, B. (2002). *Action research: Action and research.* Retrieved June 3, 2008 from http://www.scu.edu.au/schools/gcm/ar/arp/aandr.html.

Dickenson, D. K. & Brady, J.P. (2006). Towards effective support for language and literacy through professional development. In I. Martinez-Beck & M. Zaslow (Eds.) *Critical issues in early childhood professional development* (pp.141-170). Baltimore, MD: Paul H. Brooks Pub.Co.

Elliott, E. M., & Olliff, C. B. (2008). Developmentally appropriate emergent literacy activities for young children: Adapting the early literacy and learning model. *Early Childhood Education Journal,* 35(6), 551-556. doi:10.1007/s10643-007-0232-1

Engstrom, M. E., & Danielson, L. M. (2006). Teachers' perceptions of an on-site staff development model. *Clearing House,* 79(4), 170-173. doi:10.3200/TCHS.79.4.170-173

Fadde, P., & Sullivan, P. (2013). Using interactive video to develop preservice teachers' classroom awareness. *Contemporary Issues in Technology & Teacher Education,* 13(2), 1.

Foroohar, R. (2014) We've all got GM problems. *Time.* June 23, 2014.

Fullan, M. (1991). *The New Meaning of Educational Change.* London: Cassell

Gartrell, D. (2013). Guidance Matters. Democratic life skill 3: Solving problems creatively–independently and in cooperation with others. *YC: Young Children*, 68(3), 1-5

Griess, C., & Keat, J. B. (2014). Practice what we preach: Differentiating instruction and assessment in a higher education classroom as a model of effective pedagogy for early childhood teacher education candidates. *Journal of Early Childhood Teacher Education*, 35(1), 98-109. doi:10.1080/10901027.2013.874381

Harnett, J. (2012). Reducing discrepancies between teachers' espoused theories and theories-in-use: An action research model of reflective professional development. *Educational Action Research*, 20(3), 367-384.

Harwood, D., Klopper, A., Osanyin, A., & Vanderlee, M. (2013). 'It's more than Care': Early childhood educators' concepts of professionalism. *Journal of International Research & Development*, 33 (1), 4-17.

Heath, C., & Hindmarsh, J. (2002). Analysing interaction: Video, ethnography and situated conduct. In T. May (Ed.), *Qualitative research in action* (pp. 99-121). London: Sage.

Helm, J.H. (2007) Building Communities of Practice. *Young Children*, 62(4).

Helmsley-Brown, J., & Sharp, C. (2003). The use of research to improve professional practice: A systematic review of the literature. *Oxford Review of Education, 29*, 449-470.

Hidden curriculum (2014, August 26). In S. Abbott (Ed.), The glossary of education reform. Retrieved from http://edglossary.org/hidden-curriculum

Hord, S.M. (2003) Professional Learning Communities: Communities of continuous inquiry and improvement. *Issues About Change 61*, 6(1).

Hyson, M., Tomlinson, H. B., & Morris, C. S. (2009). Quality improvement in early childhood teacher education: Faculty perspectives and recommendations for the future. *Early Childhood Research & Practice (ECRP)*, 11(1).

Jalongo, M.R. & Jsenberg, J.P. (2000). *Exploring Your Role: A practitioner's guide to early childhood education*. Upper Saddle River, New Jersey: Merrill Prentice Hall.

Jensen, B., Holm, A., & Bremberg, S. (2013). Effectiveness of a Danish early year preschool program: A randomized trial. *International Journal of Educational Research*, 62115-128. doi:10.1016/j.ijer.2013.06.004.

Jones, C.R., Ratcliffe, N.J., Sheehan, H. & Hunt, G.H. (2012) An analysis of teachers' and paraeducators, roles and responsibilities with implications for professional development. *Early Childhood Education Journal*, 40 (1), 19-24.

Kagan, S. L., Britto, P.R., & Engle, P. (2005) Early learning standards: What America can learn? *Phi Delta Kappen*. 87 (5), 205-208.

Karp, N. (2006). Designing models for professional development at the local, state and National levels. In I. Martinez-Beck & M. Zaslow (Eds.) *Critical issues in early childhood professional development* (pp. 225-230). Baltimore, MD: Paul H. Brooks Pub.Co.

Kelly, V., & Rose, J. (1996). Action research and the early years of education. *Early Years*. 17(1), 41-46.

Kirkwood, D., & Beavers, E. (2013). Create an authentic, inclusive early childhood learning environment for teacher candidates. *Dimensions of Early Childhood*, 41(2), 3-9.

Kleyn, T., & Valle, J. (2014). Modeling collaborative teaching in teacher education: Preparing pre-service teachers to teach all students. *Advances in Research On Teaching*, 21137-164. doi:10.1108/S1479-368720140000021005

Knight, J., Bradley, B., Hock, M., Skrtic, T., Knight, D., Brasseur-Hock, I., & Hatton, C. (2012). Record, replay, reflect. *Journal of Staff Development*, 33(2), 18-23.

Kochan, F.K. (2000). Models for enhancing the professional development of teachers: Overview and framework. In D.J. McIntyre & D.M. Byrd (Eds.) *Research on effective models for teacher education* (pp. 1-9). Thousand Oaks, Calif: Corwin.

Landry, S., Swank, P., Anthony, J., & Assel, M. (2011). An experimental study evaluating professional development activities within a state funded pre-kindergarten program. *Reading & Writing*, 24(8), 971-1010. doi:10.1007/s11145-010-9243-1

Lattimer, H. (2012). Action Research in pre-service teacher education: Is there value added? *I.E.: Inquiry in Education*. 3(1), 001-025

Leggett, N., & Ford, M. (2013). A fine balance: Understanding the roles educators and children play as intentional teachers and intentional learners within the Early Years Learning Framework. *Australasian Journal of Early Childhood*, 38(4), 42-50.

Levin, B. (2004). Making research matter more. *Educational Policy Analysis Archives,* 12(56). Retrieved from http://epaa.asu.edu/epaa/v12n56/.

Lind, V. R. (2007). High quality professional development: An investigation of the supports for and barriers to professional development in arts education. *International Journal of Education & the Arts,* 8(2), 1.

Lino, D., (2014). The impact of teacher education on children's right to participate in their own learning. *Journal Plus Education / Educatia Plus*, 10(1), 69-76

McCann, E. J., & Turner, J. E. (2004). Increasing Student Learning Through Volitional Control. *Teachers College Record*, 106(9), 1695-1714. doi:10.1111/j.1467-9620.2004.00401.x

McNiff, J., Lomax,P., & Whitehead,J. (2000). *You and Your Action Research Project.*

New York: Routledge.

McNiff, J. (2002). *Action research for professional development.* Retrieved July 18, 2008 from http://www.jeanmcniff.com/booklet1.html

Meisels, S. J. (2011, November 29). Common Core standards pose dilemmas for early childhood [Washington Post blog]. Retrieved from http://www.washingtonpost.com/blogs/answer-sheet/post/common-core-standards-pose-dilemmas-for-early childhood/2011/11/28/gIQAPs1X6N_blog.html

Mentoring Preservice Teachers in the Preschool Setting: Perceptions of the role. (2005). *Australian Journal of Early Childhood*, 30(1), 28-35.

Mesquita-Pires, C. (2012). Children and professionals' rights to participation: a case study. *European Early Childhood Education Research Journal*, 20(4), 565-576. doi:10.1080/1350293X.2012.737242

Messenger, W. (2013). Professional cultures and professional knowledge: owning, loaning and sharing. *European Early Childhood Education Research Journal*, 21(1), 138-149. doi:10.1080/1350293X.2012.760342

Meyers, E. & Rust, F. (Eds.) (2003). *Taking action with teacher research*. Portsmouth: Heinemann.

Moloney, M. (2010). Professional identity in early childhood care and education: Perspectives of preschool and infant teachers. *Irish Educational Studies*. 29 (2). 167-187.

Mooney, C.G., (2000). *Early Childhood: An Introduction to Dewey, Montessori, Erikson, Piaget & Vigotsky*. St. Paul, MN: Redleaf Press.

Mooney, C.G., (2011) *Swinging Pendulums: Cautionary Tales for Early Childhood Education*. St. Paul, MN: Redleaf Press.

Moran, M. J. (2007). Collaborative action research and project work: Promising practices for developing collaborative inquiry among early childhood preservice teachers. *Teaching & Teacher Education*, 23(4), 418-431. doi:10.1016/j.tate.2006.12.008

Moran, M. J., Desrochers, L., & Cavicchi, N. M. (2007). Progettazione and documentation as sociocultural activities: Changing communities of practice. *Theory into Practice*, 46(1), 81-90. doi:10.1080/00405840709336552

Moyles, J. (2001). Passion, paradox and professionalism in early years' education. *Journal of International Research & Development*. 21(2), 81-95.

National Association for the Education of Young Children. (1996). *Guidelines for preparation of early childhood professionals*. Washington, DC: NAEYC.

National Association for the Education of Young Children. (2001). *Standards for early childhood professional preparation: Initial Licensure programs*. Retrieved May 5, 2011, from http;//www.naeyc.org/faculty/pdf/2002.pdf

National Association for the Education of Young Children. (2009). *Standards for early childhood professional preparation programs*. Retrieved May 8, 2011, from http;//www.naeyc.org/faculty/pdf/2009.pdf

National Governors Association Center for Best Practices, Council of Chief State School Officers (2010).*Common Core State Standards*. Washington D.C.Copyright.

Nelson, R. N. (2012). The use of video as a reflective learning tool in early childhood teacher preparation. *Annual International Conference on Education & E-Learning*, 73-76. doi:10.5176/2251-1814:EeL12.42

Nelson, S. R., Leffer, J.C. & Hansen, B.A. (2009). *Towards a research agenda for understanding and improving the use of research evidence*. Portland, OR: Northwest Regional Educational Laboratory.

Neuman, S. B. (2010). Lessons from my mother: Reflections on the national early literacy panel report. *Educational Researcher*, 39(4), 301-304. doi:10.3102/0013189X10370475

New York City Early Childhood Professional Development Institute. (2012). Core body of knowledge: New York State's core competencies for early childhood educators. (3rd ed.). Retrieved from: http://nyworksforchildren.org/Portals/o/NYWFC_Core-Body-of_Knowledge.pdf. New York, Brooklyn.

O'Brien, R. (2001). An overview of the methodological approach of action research. In R. Richardson (Ed.), *Theory and Practice of Action Research*. João Pessoa, Brazil: Universidad Federal da Paraíba. Retrieved July 15, 2008 from http://www.web.ca/~robrien/papers/arfinal.html

Pea, R. D. (1999). New media communication forums for improving education research and practice. In E. C. Lagemann & L. S. Shulman (Eds.), *Issues in education research: Problems and possibilities* (pp. 336-370). San Francisco, CA: Jossey Bass.

Persall, P., (2012). *New York State early learning alignment crosswalk.* Retrieved from: http://www.nysecac.org/files/1313/7711/9138/NYS_Early_Learning_Alignment_Crosswalk_2012.pdf

Peterson, S., Valk, C., Baker, A., Brugger, L., & Hightower, A. (2010). "We're not just interested in the work": Social and emotional aspects of early educator mentoring relationships. *Mentoring & Tutoring: Partnership in Learning*, 18(2), 155-175. doi:10.1080/13611261003678895

Picchio, M., Giovannini, D., Mayer, S. & Musatti T. (2012). Documentation and analysis of children's experience: an ongoing collegial activity for early childhood professionals. *Journal of International Research & Development.* 32(2), 159-170.

Plowman, L. (1999). Using Video for Observing Interaction in the Classroom. *Spotlight 72*, Scottish Council for Research in Education. Retrieved June 14, 2008 from http://www.scre.ac.uk/*spotlight*/spotlight72.html

Reason, P. & Bradbury, H. (Eds.). (2001). *Handbook of action research: participative inquiry and practice.* London: Sage.

Recchia, S. L., & Beck, L. M. (2014). Reflective practice as "Enrichment": How new early childhood teachers enact preservice values in their classrooms. *Journal Of Early Childhood Teacher Education*, 35(3), 203-225. doi:10.1080/10901027.2014.936074

Riel, M. (2007). *Understanding action research.* Retrieved July 25, 2008 from http://cadres.pepperdine.edu/ccar/define.html

Roberts, S., Crawford, P., & Hickmann, R. (2010). Teacher research as a robust and reflective path to professional development. *Journal of Early Childhood Teacher Education*, 31(3), 258-275. doi:10.1080/10901027.2010.500557

Robson, S. (2011). Producing and using video data in the early years: Ethical questions and practical consequences in research with young children. *Children & Society*, 25(3), 179-189. doi:10.1111/j.1099-0860.2009.00267

Roehrig, G., Dubosarsky, M., Mason, A., Carlson, S. & Murphy, B. (2011) We look more, listen more, notice more: Impact of sustained professional development on Head-Start Teachers' Inquiry based and culturally-relevant science teaching practices. *Journal of Science Education & Technology* 20 (5). 566-578.

Rogoff, B., Turkanis, C.G., & Bartlett, L., (Eds.). (2001). *Learning together. Children and adults in a school community.* New York: Oxford University Press.

Rossouw, D. (2009). Educators as action researchers: some key considerations. *South African Journal of Education*, 29(1), 1-16

Rust, F., & Clark, C., (2007). *How to do action research in your classroom: Lessons from the teachers' network leadership institute*. Retrieved from http://teachersnetwork.org/NTOL/ntol_how_to.htm

Ruto-Korir, R., & Beer, C. (2012). The potential for using visual elicitation in understanding preschool teachers' beliefs of appropriate educational practices. *South African Journal of Education*, 32(4), 393-405.

Sakellariou, M., & Rentzou, K. (2011). Cypriot pre-service kindergarten teachers' beliefs about and practices of developmentally appropriate practices in early childhood education. *Early Child Development & Care*, 181(10), 1381-1396. doi:10.1080/03004430.2010.531132

Schwartz, S. and Copeland, S. (2010). *Connecting emergent curriculum and standards in the early childhood classroom, strengthening content and teaching practices*. New York: Teachers College Press.

Scott-Little, C., Kagan, S. L. & Frelow, V.S. (2006). Conceptualization of readiness and the content of early learning standards: The intersection of policy and research? *Early Childhood Research Quarterly*, 21(2). 153-173.

Siraj-Blatchford, I., Sylva, K., Muttock, S., Gilden, R. & Bell, D. (2002). Researching effective pedagogy in the early years. Retrieved from http://www.327matters.org/Docs/RR356.pdf

Siraj-Blatchford, I., Taggart, B., Sylva, K. Sammons, P., & Melhuish, E., (2008) Towards the transformation of practice in early childhood education: the effective provision of pre-school education (EPPE) project, *Cambridge Journal of Education*, 38(1), 23 – 36.

Sleeter, C. (2014). Towards teacher education research that informs policy. *Educational Researcher*, 43(3), 146-153.

Souto-Manning, M., & Mitchell, C. H. (2010). The role of action research in fostering culturally-responsive practices in a preschool classroom. *Early Childhood Education Journal*, 37(4), 269-277. doi:10.1007/s10643-009-0345-9

Starnes, B. A. (2002). On the importance of never making it to Mars. *Phi Delta Kappan*, 83(8), 574-575.

Stemler, Steve (2001). An overview of content analysis. *Practical Assessment, Research & Evaluation, 7(17)*. Retrieved May 9, 2008 from http://PAREonline.net/getvn.asp?v=7&n=17

Stork, S., & Sanders, S. W. (2008). Physical Education in Early Childhood. *Elementary School Journal*, 108(3), 197-206. doi:10.1086/529102

Stremmel, A.J. (2002) Teacher research: nurturing professional growth through inquiry. *Young Children,* 57 (5), 62-70.

Taylor, M. J., Hallam, P. R., Charlton, C. T., & Wall, D. G. (2014). Formative assessment of collaborative teams (FACT): Development of a grade-level instructional team checklist. *NASSP Bulletin*, 98(1), 26-52.

Thornton, J. S., Crim, C.L., & Hawkins, J., (2009) The Impact of ongoing professional development program on prekindergarten teachers' professional development practices. *Journal of Early Childhood Teacher Education*, 30(2), 150-161.

Tripp, T. R., & Rich, P. J. (2012). The influence of video-analysis on the process of teacher change. *Teaching and Teacher Education, 28*, 728-739.

U.S. Department of Labor. (2007). Occupational outlook handbook: Teachers. Washington, DC. Retrieved June 27, 2008 from http://www.bls.gov/oco/ocos069.htm

Ventimiglia, L., & Reed, T. (2004). The culture of teaching. *Journal of the Association of Childhood Education International, 80*(5), 228-230.

Waite, S. & Davis, B. (2006). Collaboration as a catalyst for critical thinking in undergraduate research. *Journal of Further & Higher Education, 30*(4), 405-419. doi:10.1080/03098770600965417

Walker, R. (2002). Case study, case records and multimedia. *Cambridge Journal of Education, 32*(1), 109–127.

Walsh, D. J., Bakir, N., Lee, T. B., Chung, Y., & Chung, K. (2006). Using digital video in field-based research with children: A primer. In A. Hatch (Ed.), *Early childhood qualitative research* (pp. 43-62). New York: Routledge.

Watson, A., & McCathren, R. (2009). Including children with special needs: Are you and your early childhood program ready? *Young Children, 64*(2), 20-26.

Watson, R., & Wildy, H. (2014). Pedagogical practice of early childhood teachers: Explicit enhancement of students' literacy. *Australasian Journal of Early Childhood, 39*(2), 82-90.

Wellhousen, K., & Giles, R. M. (2005). Building literacy opportunities into children's block play: What every teacher should know. *Childhood Education, 82*(2), 74-78.

Whitebook, M. (2014). Building a skilled teacher workforce. Retrieved from http://www.irle.berkeley.edu/cscce/2014/building-a-skilled-teacher-workforce/

Whitington, V., Thompson, C. & Shore, S. (2014). 'Time to ponder': professional learning in early childhood education. *Australian Journal of Early Childhood.* 39(1), 65-72.

Wood C. (2007) Yardsticks (3rd edition) *Children in the Classroom ages 4-14.* Turners Falls: Northeast Foundation, Inc.

Zeichner, K. (2010). Competition, economic rationalization, increased surveillance, and attacks on diversity: Neo-liberalism and the transformation of teacher education in the US. *Teaching and Teacher Education, 26*, 1544-1552.

www.ingramcontent.com/pod-product-compliance
Lightning Source LLC
Chambersburg PA
CBHW081238020426
42331CB00013B/3221